Advance praise for In Trance:

"Sondra Lambert takes the reader on a journey into the intimate thoughts of her inner mind. She beautifully explains how hypnosis helped her and her family overcome traumatic events.

The book is captivating and gives the reader insight to hypnosis as a tool for self-empowerment. It clears away many misconceptions that still surround hypnosis and hypnotherapy and prevents people from benefiting from all it has to offer.

The book is beautifully written, not only for those new to the subject of hypnosis but also for practicing hypnotists who can be inspired by Sondra and Larry Lamberts' inventive hypnotic tools."

~Ina Oostrom
Designated Certified Instructor of OMNI® Hypnosis Training, Netherlands
https://www.hypnosementor.nl/

"Sondra opens her heart on theses pages. She invites you to join her in a journey of challenge, discovery, change, fulfillment and the celebration of life. Allow Sondra to take you along. You will not be left untouched."

~Daniel Arnal Romero
Hypnotist, Alicante, Spain

"*In Trance* is pure Enchantment. A masterful first-hand depiction of the experience and rewards of hypnosis! Sondra is a moving writer—with a very moving story—and she shows how hypnosis works to examine one's life and live it to the fullest. You will laugh and cry and marvel at the experience, as well as the rewards of hypnosis, as there is something In Trance for everyone who genuinely wants to reclaim or re-affirm life."

~Billy J. Shilling, MA, CH, CI, OB, CAPT USN-Ret.
Hypnotist, Springfield, Virginia

"Sondra describes how she was able to use hypnosis to unlock her Subconscious—the power of her own mind. This partnership can open up vistas of previously denied growth, healing, understanding and accomplishment. She offers to the reader a path to develop a relationship with their own subconscious to help conquer life's problems and break self-imposed barriers."

~Ralph Williams
Business Development Consultant, Washington, D.C.

"I have not read her book, but I love my Nana, so I am sure it is great!"

~Ella Lambert
Granddaughter of the author, Maryland

In
Trance

Hypnosis from the Subject's Point of View

Sondra Lambert

Cover photographs used with permission
of NaturalPhotos.tumblr.com

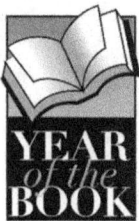

Year of the Book
135 Glen Avenue
Glen Rock, Pennsylvania 17327

ISBN 13: 978-1-942430-27-8

ISBN 10: 1-942430-27-2

Library of Congress Control Number: 2015946653

Galaxy Hypnosis has only Board Certified Hypnotists, certified by both the National Board of Hypnosis Education and Certification and the National Guild of Hypnotists. We do not attempt to treat or diagnose disease or mental disorders of any kind. Hypnosis in no way replaces standard medical procedures, but works in conjunction with them by freeing the patient of feelings or attitudes that may inhibit natural immunizing or other vital processes. Hypnosis helps to create strong mental expectancy and reduces stress, thereby normalizing the action of the autonomic nervous system. Hypnosis for certain effects or symptoms of diagnosed physical or mental illness, such as pain or addiction, requires a referral from a licensed physician or psychiatrist to determine underlying causes. Call for your free consultation and to receive a physician referral form if needed.

Dedication

I dedicate the writing of this book to my Subconscious, and to all others who will read my words, receiving inspiration through them.

The loving support of my family is of value beyond measure. Thank you and I love you absolutely: Larry Lambert, Nick Lambert, Bryan Lambert, and Rachel Duncan. Also my brother Dean Gangwer, with whom I began dreaming years ago. Our motto… "I want it all!"

Table of Contents

Foreword

Hypnosis has always been shrouded in misconception and mystery.

This is unfortunate because its benefits are vast and the experience can be so amazing! I met Sondra Lambert several years ago during a meeting of hypnosis professionals in Maryland. A newly minted Certified Hypnotist, it was obvious that her passion for her new profession was without bounds. Even then, her knowledge base was already huge because she had studied with some of the best hypnosis instructors in the world.

But there was something else about Sondra.

Most hypnotists describe trance from the outside-in—but Sondra can expertly convey the experience from the inside-out in a way that only special people can. For the vast majority of us, this is an experience, a phenomenon that is incomprehensible. For that reason alone, this should be required reading for hypnotherapists who want to gain knowledge about the inner workings of our best clients.

For the novice, or person who is wondering if hypnosis is right for them, *In Trance* offers concrete examples of how hypnotherapy can effect amazing transformations. Fewer than 5% of the people who seek out hypnotherapy have ever experienced hypnosis before, so they have many questions. Can I be hypnotized? What does hypnosis feel like? And what can hypnosis do for me?

These questions are answered in detail as Sondra explains (with personal and client examples) how and why hypnotherapy works. She describes what trance feels like and explains the methods of entering trance.

Pain management is one of the best uses of hypnosis and opens hope for our clients with chronic and acute pain. Sondra explains at length how she was able to use trance to alleviate her own acute pain associated with knee surgery and other injuries. The results were nothing short of phenomenal!

Sondra provides case studies that explain how hypnosis can be effective for weight loss, phobias, sports improvement, and other issues. Her own journey of successful weight loss using hypnosis is chronicled in detail, and since this is one of the most common issues clients have, it is especially useful. She explains how she has used this therapy to improve the lives of her clients and herself.

Sondra does not shy away from controversial topics. In fact, she gives an excellent example of using hypnotic age regression in her own growth and explains how she uses it to work with the most difficult problems for her clients.

As an expert at self-hypnosis she also explains her process for this essential skill. Finally, in the last part of the book, Sondra provides a toolkit of very helpful techniques the reader can use for personal growth.

I know you will enjoy this book as much as I did, whether you are an experienced hypnotist, a student of hypnosis, or even a prospective client who wants to know how hypnosis can help you live a better life.

Sean Michael Andrews, C.H., C.I.
Director, Atlantic Hypnosis Institute (Heidelberg, Germany)
Supervising Instructor, Dave Elman Hypnosis Institute
"The World's Fastest Hypnotist"

In Trance

Hi, my name is Sondra Lambert and you are about to read my story.

A few years ago I was introduced to hypnosis as a life changing tool. I had no idea when I had my first hypnosis session that my life would totally transform. Not knowing what to expect gave me the opportunity to evaluate on a personal level the same things you will be introduced to as you read and experience this book.

Most books on the topic of hypnosis are written by a hypnotist, for hypnotists—and most are techniques, tools, and case studies from the hypnotist's point of view.

The unfolding of life, as disclosed in these pages, is unlike anything I have read before. I share from the point of view and perspectives of the hypnosis subject:

- What is it "like" to be in hypnotic trance?
- How does it feel as a recipient?
- What happens as the process begins to move toward healing and balanced alignment?

I speak to you from within the hypnotic experience. I share healing at a level beyond thinking. Most importantly this message is shared from my heart to yours with the greatest respect. I know we are all individuals. My stories are not yours, but the path I chose can easily be customized to reflect healthy choices for you, too.

I hope to dispel the myths in such a way that enhances curiosity, interest, and opens doors for more. It is my gift to you.

I want to tell you in my own words it is *not* sleep. I want to tell you what I have heard and experienced, what I know to be my truth. I want to show you my perspective. When one issue, memory, habit, or emotion is brought up for healing, there are others who will get in line asking to be set free as well.

I want to tell you hypnosis is a mode of communication with the part of you who knows you best. I want to tell you about the profound healing which occurs when you address old wounds within a partnership with your subconscious.

Hypnosis is a consensual state of focused attention. What you focus upon is invited to shift, or change to match what fits best into your life, on an intimately personal level with swift results.

Within the pages of *In Trance*, you will be introduced to the most significant components of what is possible within the phenomena of hypnosis. It combines the expertise of a qualified hypnotist, who knows the techniques, tools, and processes to create successful positive change through the inner transformational magic of meeting, communicating, and building a solid relationship with your subconscious. This partnership will change your world, how you look at it, and what is possible when you relate within your world with fresh perspective.

This is my story. You will see me at my most vulnerable. You will see me at my most victorious. Knowing both ends of this spectrum helps us find the critical balancing points in between.

While *In Trance* is written from my personal perspective as a hypnosis subject, I am also a nationally certified hypnotist. My husband Larry and I share our professional office, Galaxy Hypnosis in Crofton, Maryland. Through this work we are blessed to help our clients build phenomenal lives in our community and now the world.

It is a good life. We live fully engaged. Living "In Trance" is the best decision I ever made—one I will never regret.

Welcome home.

You Gotta Start Somewhere

I had been spending the day with a friend when he asked me, "If you could have or do anything, what would it be?"

I told him honestly I would love to be able to release the "lock" on my throat, and the fear of having what I swallow set off a spasm in my esophagus. I had not experienced a throat spasm in years but I was tired of being careful every time I ate so it would not happen.

He looked at me, smiled and picked up the phone. This friend worked in a suite of offices which happened to include a certified hypnotherapist. He asked his colleague if he thought my "throat lock" was something which could be handled well through hypnosis.

The hypnotherapist said, "Yes, probably in one session. Tell Sondra to make an appointment."

I did.

A few weeks later, my husband Larry and I began a process that has transformed our lives. We were a bit skeptical, but have always had an adventurous spirit... plus my friend recommended it.

We arrived at the appointment with no clue that this moment was a pivotal point in our lives. The hypnotist followed the therapeutic teaching of Milton Ericson (which meant nothing to me). His office had a purple theme, Milton's favorite color. He spent a few minutes giving me a tremendous overview, telling me that my conscious thinking mind would relax and drift for a bit while he worked with my subconscious mind. I felt comfortable. When he asked me if I desired to be hypnotized by him I said, "Yes."

I did not know exactly what to expect. He sat me in a comfortable chair. On the table next to me was a box of Kleenex. *Was crying expected?*

I would hear everything he said. It was my job to just relax and follow along with the guided images he would describe. He said much of the time would be spent inviting my imagination to join us, and allowing her to bring forth the images and experiences.

I might see things, might hear things, might feel things, and he alerted me there would be some blending of memories along the way.

He made sure I knew he was watching me—monitoring my reactions—so he could shift direction as needed.

I was excited and ready to begin. The overall goal of the session was to release the protective lock in my throat from esophageal surgery a few years before.

The journey began…

He told me we were going down a lane toward a beautiful woods. I immediately found myself on the farm where I grew up in central Indiana near the woods which surrounded the barns and farm equipment. I knew this area, yet had not been there in decades.

I walked down the lane, around the old red barn and into the woods. It was a warm May afternoon. I was mushroom hunting, looking around the trunks and roots of the trees, just like when I was a kid. In my hand, I noticed a Wonder Bread bag. This particular mushroom bag was a personal memory of growing up on our family farm. I was enjoying myself so far.

He told me to look down on the ground. I would find something very special. I assumed it would be a perfect mushroom, but what I found instead was an old-time brown medicine bottle with a stopper in the top.

What an odd item to find.

I reached down to pick it up. I knew what was inside without anyone telling me. It was filled with resentment of my husband Larry. This was not the start I had expected. I felt no angst at all… just a bit surprised at what I found when I followed instructions and looked down.

At this point I knew I did not want to resent my husband, so I decided to open the bottle and dump out the contents… but no matter how hard I tried, I could not get it open.

The hypnotist kept talking and creating the scenario for my continued journey. He pointed out I was wearing a backpack, and he told me to put whatever I found inside the bag. I could stop fretting.

The scene changed. I transported myself to 26 Federal Plaza, the federal building in Manhattan where the IRS is housed. I had been there many times on business travel. I didn't even give a second's thought to the fact I had jumped from my childhood backyard woods in Indiana straight to downtown New York City. All in a day's work. I do not even recall what was suggested that made this jump, yet there I was.

Next he said something like, "Okay now, in front of you is a body of water."

If any of you have ever been to 26 Fed Plaza, you know there's no water anywhere. The power of suggestion was so smooth, I turned around to find a stone fountain, right there at street level in front of the stairs. *Wow, how convenient. Suggest to see water and water appears!*

(Now at this point you may be wondering what the hell does any of this have to do with my throat? I did not know either but I was having fun!)

I was asked to walk over to the water and notice it was very cloudy, almost muddy. *Yep, muddy fountain water. Got it.*

He called my attention to the sound of a bird. I looked for it, and just as you might expect since I was on the street in Manhattan, the bird was a pigeon. *This hypnosis stuff is cool.*

5

The bird was trapped. In the blink of an eye, at the speed of thought, I was standing in my current backyard looking into my bunny thicket in the corner—and there was a beautiful yellow bird trapped inside. Poof the pigeon became a canary.

I remember thinking, *Well, this is not cool.* Now I had a bottle of resentments I couldn't open and a bird stuck in my thicket. I was really quite concerned for the bird. The momentum was rolling.

The hypnotist's voice suggested for me to turn around. When I did, he said, I would be looking into the face of unconditional love.

Okay, forget the bird.

I turned to see running toward me—through the back door and across the patio—my grandson, arms wide open, shouting, "NANA!"

In that moment, I knew the sight, the sound and the feeling of unconditional love. It flooded through me as nothing I had ever felt before. I hugged him with my entire being. I could have stayed there forever, however the trance time moved on, so did I too.

I stood back up. The backpack I was wearing had become quite heavy. I had been collecting things at each stop along the way. It was getting uncomfortable, and the hypnotist suggested it would be better if I just got rid of it.

He asked me to stand very still and realize an angel was approaching me. I looked up to see the angel who played Earl on the television show "Saving Grace." Earl and I were standing on my patio. He opened his wings and wrapped them around me. *Oh my God!* To be wrapped in the arms of my very own angel. He was in no hurry.

Part of me felt like crying, part of me felt like laughing, and all of me stood there in awe filled with wonder. I was protected from anything and everything at that moment. God, it felt good. My angel just held me, rubbed my hair and chuckled a bit. I guess I was not his first hug, but he was mine and he knew it.

No words were shared. They were not necessary. The open communication from his heart to mine was fully functioning. It was okay, they were not needed.

I *felt* more than *heard* him ask me if I was ready to remove the weight of the burdens I had collected. They were heavy. He offered to lift my burdens, to carry away whatever was in that backpack and whatever else I was willing to give up. Could it really be that easy? The peace I felt consumed me. No words came. I just looked into his angelic eyes and nodded my head YES.

Earl reached around my shoulders. He lifted the heavy backpack. At the speed of thought he flipped it out of the picture. My burdens were just gone. Poof!

I felt lighter. I had no definition for what I had just let go of.

In a whoosh of emotions, I was so grateful I had not opened the old brown bottle of past resentments. I had not wanted to look at them, but thought I had to in order to get rid of them. Instead, I just left them bottled up. My Earl angel took them away.

Thank you, Earl.

It was time to begin bringing this session full circle and finish everything that had been set in motion. Earl hugged me and said he would be with me forever. The trusted connection we had made was mine to keep. That was when I think I started to cry. This level of unconditional love with benefits consumed me, heart and soul.

I was back to 26 Fed Plaza at the fountain. All the burdens were now gone and the water was clear. I reached down into that water to locate the items that had been hidden earlier by the murky water. I was surprised to see laying in the clear fountain water my DOT ID badge on the lanyard my daughter made for me. This obviously was a message about my job and the struggles within it.

I had been passed over more than once for an inner-office upgrade from contractor to federal employee. My way of handling this disappointment (and the blow to my ego) was to draw back, to do the job I was being paid to do only. I stopped helping everyone with extra office things. I had become a punch the clock employee and my job had lost its shine.

When I looked into that fountain and saw my bright shiny ID badge, the message I received was, "Sondra, go back to work. Get over yourself. The resentment and pain were stored in the backpack. It's gone now and you can get back to work with great joy."

Get on with your life because it's a phenomenal one.

I reached into the water, took my lanyard and put it around my neck. Wow, I felt better. I had no idea that was even in there.

In the blink of an eye I was back in my yard again. I turned to the bird who, although trapped in the thicket, was not struggling. I reached up to free her. When I moved my hand, I discovered she was already free. She was never actually trapped. It had been an illusion for my benefit. I watched this beautiful bird fly away singing as she dipped and soared into the wind. I knew her freedom was a symbol of my own.

I walked back through the woods, casually looking for mushrooms and finding them in abundance. The journey had gone through my entire life, from the unconditional love gifted to me in the form of my precious grandson, and a visit from my very own angel who easily carried my burdens away. A release of bottled up resentments of my husband gone. I felt free, exhilarated.

My hypnotist congratulated me on my phenomenal journey and said, "Before I bring you back into my office, there is one more thing we need to accomplish. In your hand is a key, and this key will unlock your throat from all remaining limitations. With the rest of you so free it is now time for your throat to receive her freedom as well."

I took the key. He counted from three down to one. When he got to "1," I turned the key and physically felt my throat accept her freedom from fear of residual trauma.

When I returned to full awareness I had a Kleenex in my hand. It had been held tightly for quite some time.

I want you to notice that within this session he did not tell me what to do, what to think, or what to heal. He just simply took me on a journey, and along the way, I collected the things which needed to be dealt with. I was unaware of what was happening until it was time for Earl to remove the weight of the backpack. I was walking, allowing an inner healing to take its path. I walked through all that I had accomplished… with victory at every step.

He asked me how long I thought our session had taken. I answered, "Probably ten minutes." I had been in trance for about an hour. Time was just suspended while I was exploring and discovering.

I was so charged up and more than excited.

In one hour, I had unraveled a lifetime of crap. I had no concept that another sixty minutes would incredibly alter my life's path.

Now years later, I am a certified hypnotist with a passion to assist others on their journey—with equal respect for being the escort, the assistant with a toolbox as big as my heart.

Hello, Subconscious

The intention of this book is to share with you from a very personal perspective the flow of experiences I have encountered, and how I have met and grown to partner with my subconscious. Hypnosis introduced me to an entire portion of my identity I was meeting for the first time.

It goes something like this…

"Settle in. Settle down and relax. With every breath, allow your mind, body, and all that you are to drift, to float, and to dream. With every breath, relax, allowing the relaxation to flow through you, from the top of your head to the tips of your toes.

"Give yourself permission to release the grip you have on anything you perceive as solid or absolute, allowing relaxation to carry you farther on the perfect cloud, into the blue black of space. As you relax, the better you will feel; the better you feel, the more you will relax. It truly is just that simple.

"Drift, float, dream. As you settle in, settle down and relax. The relaxation you feel is yours to keep. All you need to do is listen to the sound of my voice and follow my very simple instructions."

I settled in, I settled down, and I relaxed. I drifted, I floated, and I dreamed. I gave myself permission to listen to the sound of his voice and follow his simple instructions. I could hear the sounds of life around me, but they gave me comfort, knowing I had not gone anywhere.

I opened my eyes to see fingers moving asking me to imagine a butterfly, flitting and floating then darting toward my eyes, then away. My eyes grew tired and heavy, the butterfly was just fine. *Enjoy the flight*, I thought.

I imagined standing at the top of a grand staircase. As if by magic, I could see them, feel them, and was more than ready to journey down them. The count down the stairs was simple, each step a number. Each number came with an invitation for relaxation, comfort, and a disconnection from any distraction. This was tremendous.

At the bottom of the stairs was a landing that led to a door. I knew this door was special; I had come to the entrance of an environment within me, the innermost parts of who I am, my subconscious. I stood at this door feeling safe, feeling secure. I saw a door. I knew I held the only key, and since I create adventure mixed with anticipation at every moment, I was excited. I reached into my pocket for the key. As you might expect it fit perfectly.

The key fit into the lock with such smooth ease, it truly was like coming home. The door swung open and I stepped into a room which was familiar, yet fresh and new. I walked around knowing I had just come into contact with a part of me who was ready to share this journey of exploration and discovery. I had come home to myself.

There were a couple of comfy couches so I walked over and sat down. I could hear my hypnotist clearly. Following his simple instructions was easy, however this moment was so surreal that his involvement seemed to be detached. I looked up to see a beautiful younger slimmer and trimmer Sondra sitting near me. I remember exactly what she was wearing.

I knew at that moment, right then and there, I was at a pivot point. I would never forget. Boy, was I right!

It was the first time I heard the phrase "Hello, Subconscious," and she responded. It was interesting because my subconscious had never been invited to speak before, so when we first began she gave one-word thoughtful answers. Plenty of "yes" and "no" until she realized that open communications were not only okay but encouraged.

We had to co-create a communication system that could be used by both of us. What we came up with was a thought-based question and answer process. I would think or ask a question. Magically a simple word or image or memory would come into my thoughts. Without much trouble we began to communicate.

I asked her what name I should call her. Instantly I knew that her name was Intuition. I recognized that her body shape and size were well balanced and she was healthy, strong, intelligent. She had a humor that allowed me to be comfortable and she was so pleased to be recognized, acknowledged.

It was easy to form a partnership with Intuition. She has been with me my entire life. She knew me better than I knew myself and it was perfectly clear that she was fiercely loyal. Unlike me, she did not seem to have any self-esteem issues. Intuition was strong and capable. I liked her.

There were questions being asked of her while I listened to her answers.

"Subconscious, what do you do for Sondra?"

Intuition said she is the one who holds all of the details, much like an office manager with unlimited resources. She had access to all of the stored "stuff." When requested to do so, she could give a full account of any inquiry.

"Subconscious, what is your relationship with Sondra?"

Intuition responded. "Sondra is my responsibility. We are a team. I will fight with her, or I will fight *for* her. Sondra is my very heart and I love her. Now that we have made this connection, I know that all things are possible. I can and will answer her questions. I can and will assist her in understanding things from a much deeper level. I am her best friend. I am her confidante and she can discuss anything with me. I am the spark that lights her flame. And most importantly I am not alone."

"Does she listen to you?"

Intuition answered. "Sondra has a keen awareness of the world around her, so it is possible to whisper to her in the wind, or remind her of a memory using something in her vision fields. She has never before realized how close we are, or the limitless resources available. Does she listen to me? Yes, at a very elementary level within what she has known up until now. That is about to change."

Intuition shared her willingness to begin fresh. Her enthusiasm was contagious.

"Do you realize you can effect change within her such as how she perceives her outside world experiences? You hold and act out her imaginations, correct?"

Intuition spent quite some time with this question and required a great deal of assistance from my hypnotist. It was like a light bulb came on.

"Oh wow, yes. I can ease a fear because I know she truly has nothing to be afraid of. Sondra's perception of a memory need not concern her in such a way. I know that every nerve is connected to every other nerve, therefore I can shift things around for her."

Intuition loved being gifted with an intensity knob. This was my first hypnotic tool. The knob is simple and works at the speed of thought. When attention to detail requires or desires focused attention, the knob is turned up. When the situation or the circumstance nears an unnecessary tipping point, the knob can be turned down. This is a shared tool (as they all are) between the conscious thinking mind and the working subconscious mind.

Intuition and I spent all afternoon getting acquainted and choosing how we would continue to be friends. We opened a clear communication flow using her multipurpose systems. My hypnotist patiently gave us time to realize the magic that was happening, yet was astute enough to know when it was time to ask another question to keep the session flowing. He knew what was happening was precious. He also knew that he was the guide. His assistance was absolutely mission critical. This path was fresh, new, and he was helping us create the guidelines to move into a brand new world.

It was clear, what we had started that day would continue to be built upon after the session was complete. He gave several excellent suggestions of "where to go from here" and an invitation to return anytime. The hypnotist's role had been absolutely necessary to set things in motion, but I was able to go home with confidence.

Intuition and I began at a steady pace. We figured out what would work best and we practiced daily. I would talk out loud. She would respond with clear thoughts. I would think instead of speak when around other people.

Our favorite times together became my drive home from Washington, D.C., each business day. Twenty-two miles that (before this point) had been a tiresome trek through commuter traffic gave me a captive audience with Intuition. And her with me.

I would ask her to show me things, and she did. I would ask her to bring up thoughts which would serve me better to see from a different perspective, and she did. I would talk to her about memories and the effect they had on me, and she would point out some detail or point of view I had not realized.

We developed a routine on our afternoon drive. When I got to a particular intersection close to home, I would ask her what I needed to "work" on today. A thought or a discarded responsibility would come to mind. When I got home I would give it my attention—immediately before doing anything else. We realized that if I picked up on her guidance just three miles from home, I would follow through, whereas if she waited to give it to me once I got home the momentum of life got in the way.

Intuition became my best friend. She helped me love myself. Her point of view was simple: "I love you, so you might as well love me too since we are spending so much time together."

Throughout the years that have followed, we have learned to communicate and build our relationship without being escorted into hypnotic trance. We both enjoy the concept of useful hypnotic tools, though, and they always assist us on our journey.

Hypnosis provides a smooth and loving path to what is always available.

Is it required? No, it's not.

Would I trade it for anything else in the entire world? No way!

Meet the Inners

One of the first things I came to realize when I met my Subconscious (whom I named Intuition) was that she does not know it all.

That came as a shock.

When I asked her where I left my necklace, she didn't seem to know. *Oh man, I've got this all wrong. I thought she was the keeper of my knowledge. I thought she knew everything!*

In true Sondra fashion I asked to be hypnotized to figure out what was going on. It was fascinating to watch Intuition at work. I watched and listened from my seat on the comfy couch while my hypnotist took me into trance and asked her to come forward.

He started by asking her how memories are stored.

She showed me something that looked like a fax machine where she could request information and it would be brought forth to her. It was connected to what looked like a secure warehouse, filled with all my knowledge and awareness.

He asked how her archive system worked.

She laughed and led us to a door in my apartment (that up until that moment I had never realized was there). I went into this new room, looked around and knew the shelves were filled with the objects and items of my life. They were all rather blurry, obscured from clear sight.

I felt the presence of someone who seemed to be a curator of my little life museum. She could bring up any object I wanted to share an experience with. I had been enjoying watching the show "Warehouse 13" of the SYFY channel. After seeing this room, I decided I had my own warehouse and a Claudia to take care of my stuff. Subconscious used a TV show to make something clear within my understanding.

Just for fun I asked to see the Chatty Cathy doll I got for Christmas when I was seven. There she was on the table in front of me. She had the pull-string at the back of her neck and her blue dress was covered in cake batter. (That Christmas I had also gotten an Easy Bake Oven!)

I thanked my version of Claudia and knew I could come back into this memory archive anytime. She would assist in finding whatever I wanted to spend time with.

Wait a minute!! I thought. *Intuition is not alone in here.* She has help. She has company. There's more to me than I realized.

And a new quest began to find out who else was in there.

From a hypnotist's point of view one of the most amazing techniques, championed by Roy Hunter, is called parts therapy. What I'm going to share next is the Sondra version with a major twist.

The life we choose to live in the thinking world is so multifaceted. We play a multitude of roles. At any given time I am mom, wife, daughter, sister, friend, hypnotist... you get the idea.

Well take a moment and imagine that within yourself there are similar role systems in place. Each has its own purpose and they work together for your greatest good.

I had a curator who took care of my life history museum. We asked Intuition if she had others with her to assist in the life balance of Sondra.

She said, "Yes!"

We decided to call these precious ones "Inners." So when you read about me working with one of my Inners this is where that concept was created.

The concept was born and I have built upon it ever since. There is a willingness for the Inners to create ebb and flow within me. I use this connection to the depths of me in tremendously powerful ways.

For most of my life, I have battled issues with self-image.

One day my husband Larry helped me communicate with an Inner who refused to look into the mirror. He asked her what her name was and all he got was a shoulder shrug. She told him she felt ugly and did not like to look at herself. He asked if she was an Inner of Sondra.

She replied, "Well of course, Sondra hasn't looked in a mirror for years."

He asked her if she would like a name, and she smiled at him and said yes. He asked if he could choose a name for her. Again she said yes. He told her he was going to give her a name that reflected what he saw when he looked at her.

He named her Beauty.

Meeting the Inners continued. Larry kept working with me. He liked calling out "the part of Sondra that works with her body shape and size."

This was an Inner who is the physically fit Sondra. She wears a workout outfit. Her name became Image.

Image is bold and strong and likes to exercise. *How convenient.* We talked with Image and asked her if she wanted to stay in the apartment.

She said yes, and she also wanted to be Beauty's sister. They decided to share a room.

Voilà! Beauty and Image became sisters on a shared mission. Image helped Beauty look in the mirror and even took her to sit for her portrait that now hangs on the wall. At first that painting was covered with a velvet drape in my subconscious's apartment, but now the image hangs unobstructed.

As you may have guessed, "Thinking Sondra" no longer has a hang-up about mirrors.

Another Inner who came forward was a young girl we named "Teen Sondra." She showed up unannounced and said very little. She hung out, did not disturb, and did not seem to have a purpose.

In a hypno session we interviewed her. She was the persona within Sondra who had been traumatized at age 16 when her home life shattered. She felt she'd been caught in the middle of an impossible situation. She had shown up in our session for some help, but didn't know who to talk to or how to ask.

"Highness," the top of my management team, took her in. Like magic, the healing of a broken kid began.

Was it easy? No, but it was accomplished brilliantly.

When "Teen Sondra" was on her feet and the healing complete, we asked if she wanted to stay.

She said she didn't have anywhere to go back to. She wanted to stay. So "Princess" (my fun-loving younger self) offered her a new name, and "Glory" now lives among us.

Some Inners are just internal systems that have been given names to create a family atmosphere within my inner living environment. Others have come from healing moments such as "Teen Sondra."

One such Inner is "10." When Sondra was 10 years old, something happened to her that was kept in a closed memory until she was in a safe enough situation to remember it.

I'd had glimpses of the "incident" for years but none of the pieces ever quite fit together. There was no need to poke or prod. Leaving it alone seemed just fine.

Then one day "10" showed up, and it was time to love this kid into peace, calm, joy, and ease.

She was not traumatized but did required a mind-level rescue from where she'd been hiding. With the assistance of several sessions "10" stepped into a safe place. We created a playground for her.

She is not a functioning level within Sondra, but rather a rescued kid who is now safe to play and be a child again.

The final Inner I would love to introduce you to is "8."

I had a hypnosis session with someone who regressed me back to a time in life that was all good. An eight-year-old Sondra came forward, and she was just delightful. Life was good, playing was easy, and everything had always been okay.

This beautiful girl "8" asked to stay after the session to hold Sondra's hand and tell her that everything would be okay. It always has been. She is such a cute kid. I cannot begin to tell you the number of times "Thinking Sondra" has been stressed and "Intuition" sent over "8" to hold her hand. *Pure gold!*

New Normal

What happens when everything changes?

You are now invited to watch the process I took to step into my "new normal"… more times than I care to count.

I may phrase it differently, or embrace it from a multitude of directions, but at its core my message is, "It's okay for life to change, and to enjoy the journey."

From almost the first moment I was excited to look at things differently. Acceptance made it possible for me to view a situation and allow it to morph into something I had not considered before.

Shifting into a "new normal" means I no longer needed to remember the "old normal." My subconscious—who holds all of my memories—simply says, "Okay, we've got something new here," while I continue living my life to the fullest.

I don't recall learning to ride a bike. I just know that at some point, I found my balance. I have no requirement to remember the details. It is sufficient to simply know that I can.

Hypnosis is a partnership with your subconscious, which allows you the freedom to process issues or challenges, knowing that she has you covered. There is no need for you to try to keep it all straight. No notes or study materials required. One of the supreme gifts of hypnosis is that because you are not required to remember, you can choose to forget.

It is a choice.

Change happens quickly when you give yourself the freedom to let go of burdens and flow into the newness of well-being, health, healing, and wholeness.

When you are invited to loosen your grip, the grip also lets go of you. You may ask yourself who was holding onto whom?

It doesn't matter.

When you and the issue both release your strangle hold, everyone wins. Instead of tension and anger, fill your open hands with gratitude.

Change is scary. We may wonder, "Who am I," if we do not have our problems, our issues, and our challenges to keep us company.

What will I talk about? Who will I become? How will my identity shift or change?

These are big questions and the choices and possibilities may just surprise you.

Imagine for a moment you are witnessing an elaborate domino run being tipped. You watch it race quickly with an excitement that can only be described as awe. Each tile is close enough to tip the next—unless someone or something creates a gap—at which point the run ends. We can always create gaps so that change comes in smaller portions. Regardless of the pace or the place, the excitement comes in anticipation of what's next.

Once the first domino was tipped for me I have watched and experienced my hypnotic run with amazement. Over and over again I have stepped into a position of celebrating a "new normal."

The old is gone, the new has come.

Had I stopped with the first domino I would have missed *everything* else that has happened since then.

I encourage you to embrace the possibility. Will you tip the first domino?

Setting the Cruise Controls

I was learning quickly, having a blast, and I knew that I wanted to experience more. I wanted to get better acquainted with myself from the inside out.

One of the things I learned is when I am in trance I can see, hear, and feel. I *see* as if in video, I *hear* within my mind, and *feel* clear emotional signals as well.

During one of my early sessions it was suggested that I imagine a still calm lake. I went to the salt mines in Bavaria with the lake inside the mountain. There was no tide nor movement. It was lit by torches on the walls with the shadows glistening across the water.

I was asked to consider my entire life ahead of me, and it could be any future I chose.

The emotion of hope flooded through me. A feeling of forward momentum surrounded me. I saw the tip of a giant pyramid pointed into the lake with the bulk of the structure expanding into all the world around me. My interpretation of this moment signified I was standing at the starting point to the rest of my life. There was nothing but potential ahead of me.

I take a breath now as I type these words. I still feel the thrill of fresh insight for my life.

I left those initial sessions wondering where the adventure would take me next. I had begun with a request for my throat to release. That had been handled promptly on day one. The hunger to know myself better from the inside out became a desire beyond description.

I had been gifted with the ability to meet myself at my very core and even though at that point I had not started to talk with my subconscious in conversational style, I still knew the best was yet to come. I wanted to get to know her even more.

I wondered what else was possible. As I looked at my life, I tried to decide which areas were best suited for hypnosis.

Present-day Sondra might hold up a sign to Past-day Sondra: "Watch out what you ask for. You may just get it!"

Larry and I had been married more than 30 years. We raised our three kids, and our lives were now our own. We decided to go on a cruise. It would be a week in the Caribbean.

I started thinking this would be a ship filled with gorgeous and well-proportioned babes.

Self-image issues began to make me uncomfortable, again. Though this might be the trip of a lifetime, I suddenly needed mental assistance so I wouldn't get onboard and hide in my room all week.

Enter my secret weapon!

I wondered if hypnosis could help me get ready for the cruise. Larry and I did some hypnotist shopping and found someone who didn't live too far away and asked if he would be willing to have a session with a lady who hoped to enjoy her vacation, minus the baggage of self-image issues.

Enter into my life Todd Stevens, a man who to this day continues to be a close friend.

My request was clear. I wanted to go on this cruise and make it a trip worth remembering.

Todd's hypnotic pre-talk was a hoot and two hollars. We were able to establish that what I was actually asking for was a series of post-hypnotic suggestions—triggers set within me—that could be activated later by my husband Larry. He explained clearly that he would create these suggestions and triggers and then hand the controls over to Larry to establish the full effect.

Todd was the first hypnotist to say to me, "Listen to the sound of my voice and follow my simple instructions." Over the next few hours we set up a myriad of hypnotic suggestions that would enhance our marriage, create an atmosphere of extreme responsiveness, and allow my husband and I to celebrate our intimate relationship to an infinite degree.

Let me just say it was clearly a new frontier. Todd smiled and said, "Larry, buddy, I think my work here is done. She's all yours."

With these triggers in place, my husband of over 30 years had me climbing the walls. And I no longer had any concerns about the other babes who would be onboard. This would be about us. Larry and I went on the cruise, and had the time of our lives. He would use a trigger phrase in public (knowing how I would react), and we laughed like kids and loved the nights away.

Now if I had not been hooked on hypnosis before… I asked myself, "If this is possible, then what else??"

Todd had set my cruise controls, and handed Larry the keys to a brand new life with his wife.

Larry In Trance

After our cruise we returned to Todd for an update. Larry had been experiencing the positive results hypnosis had added to our lives, and he decided he needed to do some "research" and see what it was like to experience it personally.

We regaled Todd with stories of our phenomenal cruise fun, and had more than one laugh at how significant his prep session had been for us.

He and Larry then had a long talk about the phenomena of hypnosis and the significant shifts and changes Larry had seen in me since we began my hypnosis journey.

My husband is a very intellectual thinker and although he was interested in experiencing hypnosis, he was also on alert to pay careful attention to the process and technique so he could recall it cognitively and talk about it intelligently with Todd when they finished.

Todd was more than up for the challenge of hypnotizing this truly remarkable man... who had more curiosity than desire to *relax*.

Larry decided his request for the session would be to increase his ability to focus on tasks when the world around him was quite active. He also wanted to work a bit with memory and short-term goals.

Because Todd had hypnotized me before (and I was sitting in the chair right beside Larry), he let me know it would be fine for me to go into trance and just follow along. Although he would be talking directly to Larry, I could and would benefit by listening to the sound of his voice.

The induction was simple and the session went well. He walked Larry through a focusing ring exercise which invited him to place a "ring" around "anything" with his concentrated effort. Unless something else was expected or held a higher priority, Larry would pay it no significant attention.

Larry could shift the contents of what he placed within the ring at will. This would become a permanent tool for his needs when focus in a hectic world was necessary.

That's when Todd suggested a memory tool that would significantly shift the theme and outcome of the rest of our afternoon.

He called this exercise "the cottage of memories." Through a short guided meditation he invited Larry to take a walk. A cottage came into view. "Walk towards it and realize you have the only key. Now open the door and step inside. Within the room is a very special chair. Have a seat!"

As Larry sat down, Todd explained the room was full of all of Larry's adult memories: sights, sounds, smells.

"Go ahead, look around a bit, get comfortable. Now realize that at your right hand is a button, and as you push that button, everything in this room, all memories and everything hooked onto them will be sucked into the bottom of your chair. It's a special sort of washing machine. Now pull the lever and the process of washing all those memories will begin."

Settle in, settle down, and relax. It's about to get weird. The room shifted from a museum collection to a clear space.

What happens when all of your memories take a bath? We were about to find out.

"While the memory washing is being accomplished, realize there is a door across the room. Stand up and go through that door. There is a second room filled with all your teenage memories. And what a surprise… there is another very special chair. Have a seat and repeat the process. Watch all those memories get sucked into the bottom of your chair as you push the button. Pull the lever to begin the washing and cleansing process."

There had been no requirement to examine anything. Subconscious could oversee the laundry.

"But look across the room… another door. Let's go! The third room is filled with all of your childhood memories… same chair… same process…"

Todd told Larry his memories were being cleansed and they would soon be available to be seen with fresh eyes and from a fresh perspective. They would appear as the same general experience… minus any negative residue or connected baggage that had been ready to fall away or be released.

"So now it's time to reclaim those memories. There is another button on the side of your chair. As you push that button, your childhood memories will return to the room. Notice they are clearer, more defined. They are no longer hiding behind the crap that previously obscured them."

The button pushed, the memories returned, and the water beneath the chair was flushed away and gone forever. Goodbye to the distractions and crud.

"Now look at your memories with fresh eyes. See what you have not seen in a very long time. Memories return with higher definition and greater clarity. What else had been happening at those moments that until now were hidden?"

Goodbye, distractions. Hello, fresh perspective.

"Now it's time to walk back into your teen room and repeat this phenomenal process. Push the button. *Voilà!* Your teen memories are fresh, cleaned up and amazingly clear. Flush away the dirty water. Gone forever…"

Gone forever.

"Back to the adult memories room. Sit in the chair. Are you ready for the life you are living right here, right now to come into better focus, to be freshly cleaned up?"

Larry said yes.

"Okay, press the button. Flush and allow your memories to return to this room, strong, clear and dynamic."

The next suggestion was simple.

"This amazing cottage is yours to return to you anytime you choose. You can visit, comb through—and learn from—these memories at your leisure, any time. You will notice many things that you will now see in a different light. Your perspective is invited to shift and change. Obstacles have been obliterated and you have an invitation to see your life fresh and new."

Todd brought Larry back out of trance to get a general impression, followed by a rather lively discussion. Todd offered to show Larry another hypno tool/technique. The session was going great and these two friends were enjoying the collaboration.

Todd asked Larry to think of a memory he would like to look at from a fresh perspective. "Not a train wreck, just something you want to shift a bit."

Remember that I'm still sitting in the chair beside Larry, taking all this in like a sponge. My own subconscious was highly active. They were not talking to me but I was not missing a thing.

The suggestion was to bring up a memory, take a snapshot, turn the memory into a single photo. This picture was in vivid color with great detail.

"Take a moment to ponder the essence of what you learned from this event. Now you have a gold pen in your hand, write one word or phrase across the front of the photo which best describes the lesson learned. Place this picture in a frame. As you hold the frame in your hands, slowly watch the color drain from it, shifting the image and the memory to grayscale.

"With the framed memory now viewed as shades of gray and the lesson learned plainly written across it, stand up and place it on the wall directly behind you. You can turn back around, knowing it's still there—but it is clearly *behind* you with no need to keep it in the forefront ever again."

There is peace and freedom in placing the past behind you. So powerful.

What happened next would rock my world and set me free. What I did not see coming would consume me, then bring me out the other side… healed and whole for the first time in 15 years.

Freedom in the Trauma Center

After a lengthy session, Todd stepped out of the room for a few moments. While he was gone I looked at my husband Larry and we knew instantly this was an opportunity for me to let go of a nightmare-level memory.

Todd returned to the room. I asked him if it was possible to go back to a traumatic memory with awareness of how things eventually turned out— in order to heal.

He smiled and simply said, "Sure."

My reaction was spontaneous, relief mixed with grief. Todd had no clue what box had just been opened.

We talked a moment about the tool he had just given Larry for draining the color from an event or situation and putting it on the wall behind you.

He reminded me that his first suggestion was to choose something that was *not* a train wreck.

Okay, so that tool wasn't right for this situation.

One of the challenges I had faced for a decade and a half was the fact that at age 17, our oldest son Nick experienced a massive stroke. Larry had been deployed with the US Army in support of NATO during the crisis in Bosnia. It would take a full 24 hours before Larry could be located and transported back home to a military base in Worms, Germany.

For all those years, I had held Larry somehow accountable... thinking that if he had been there things would have turned out differently.

I began to tell Todd the framework of what happened to our son on July 13, 1995. He had collapsed while playing ultimate frisbee, had been transported to the local German hospital trauma center, and placed on total life support.

For someone who did not see this coming, Todd looked intrigued and more than willing to help me. His agenda for the day had just been radically modified.

The stroke was a life-altering event with multiple adjustments—some of which had lingering effects. Coping skills do not automatically shut off when they are no longer needed. At least they had not for me. Life had moved on while we lived our lives fully.

But now I had an opportunity to heal. And I had no idea what to ask for.

One memory had haunted me. It was the moment I desired to go back and remove pressure from—the period I called "the trauma center."

Since my English-speaking son Nick was in a German hospital, they could not communicate with him freely. Family members are not usually invited into that area, but it was imperative someone be with him to calm him down. Although he was not coherently responsive he was highly agitated and fighting whatever space he was trapped within.

I walked into the room. Nick was laying on a trauma bed. Staff members were working with him. The lights were intensely bright, machines everywhere, people scurrying quickly and shooting me sympathetic glances… yet not looking me in the eye.

The doctor told me one side of Nick's body presented as paralyzed. They felt he had experienced a stroke.

A stroke? My 17-year old son, a champion high school wrestler, who runs cross-country like a champ? What was happening? The world as I knew it had gone crazy.

At that moment something occurred which seared into my entire being for the next 15 years. It visited me in my dreams usually escorted in a flood of tears.

Nick opened his eyes and looked at me. Absolutely terrified, he was in a state of pure panic.

And there was nothing I could do for him.

The message in my son's eyes said, 'I am about to die. I'm scared, Mom. Help me.'

There was nothing I could do for my precious son. He knew he was going to die. I knew he was going to die. Yet all we could do—at least for that moment—was look into each other's eyes and say, "I love you."

Things after that moved at lightning speed. Nick was transported to ICU and placed on total life support.

Todd listened to my story and talked to me. He would intentionally escort me back to that moment so I could talk to Nick with the knowledge I now have, after the facts of that night moved forward.

He explained "Regression to Cause"—to be escorted back to a past moment in time with the knowledge we now have and make peace, or heal, or whatever needs to be dealt with. He shared that he would be my escort; all I needed was a desire for it to be successful, to be willing to listen to the sound of his voice, and to follow his simple suggestions. If things got to be too intense, he would and could adjust his choice of words to bring about positive change by shifting and changing my point of view.

I laid down with Larry beside me. It was very important to me that for this time he was with me. Larry held my hand throughout the entire session and it gave me strength.

Todd asked if there was anything else I felt important for him to know, and then asked me to close my eyes.

The feeling, the process, the pathway of going into hypnotic trance is so very soothing to me. Subconscious was invited to come upfront while I drifted, floated, and dreamed of a safe neutral place. It is not a case of disappearing or becoming unaware, it is instead a moment of focused attention. I knew Todd's voice and I trusted his skills as he took me back into this painful moment. It was weird to return to a past moment in time, yet knowing it was only a visit allowed me to enter with a purpose of healing instead of the "Oh my God, I can't breathe" norm.

Todd did not have to go digging for the moment to regress to. After I was settled and open to take the journey, I was "transported" back to the hospital, the trauma center, the room where Nick lay dying. It was as if I was actually there again, the sights the sounds. But this time the emotions were a bit different. I felt safer and more solid, which I attributed (at the time) to the fact that Larry was holding my hand.

We did not need to look around or access the situation; we all knew exactly why I was there. Todd simply said, "Sondra, with the knowledge you have now, talk to your son."

There was Nick lying on the table with his terrified eyes looking to me for comfort. But *this time* I was able to give him some.

And I cried. My God, I cried through the entire session. The tears of a grieving mother about to tell her son that everything is gonna be alright.

I began, "Son, you are going to be okay. You do not die tonight. You are going to go to sleep for about a week, but you will wake up. When you do I will be there. You will call me mom and after three weeks you will walk out of this place, get in your car and your dad will drive you home. This is going to be one of the worst nights of our lives, but, honey, I promise you… look at me, Nick! Everything is going to be okay. It is all right if you do not understand what is being said around you; they are speaking German. Your dad and I will be with you the entire time you are sleeping and I promise you, son, you are going to be OK!"

I told my beloved son that he would reach his thirties, he would be married to Wendy, and have a daughter Talia, and a son Joshua, and a life in San Antonio, Texas, working for the water department. I told him he would own his own house, his cars, and have a dog.

I cried the tears of a mom with a broken heart who'd been given the opportunity to right what I had perceived as a wrong... by not encouraging him the first time.

Todd and Larry stayed very close to me, and between the two of them they led me through a series of opportunities to let go of the heaviness.

My mission was accomplished. I felt "better."

Todd asked me if I was finished and I told him, "I think so."

He grinned and said that if we needed to go back in later we could, but for now, it seemed right to return to the present.

It sounded good to me. I was tired and felt the weight of my son's life ease off my shoulders. A nightmare of magnitude had been released.

Before returning, Todd invited me to tell Nick (and more importantly myself) once more that everything turns out okay. He told me to back out of the room, shut off the lights, and close the door. I never ever had to go back in the room again. My subconscious agreed with him that a profound healing was being processed.

I had gone back into that horrible night, and though the circumstances were the same, the way I handled it shifted. Because I was invited to work within my memories and could step away from the intensity of the moments, instead of looking into my son's eyes as he was dying, I looked into them and told him he was going to LIVE. And live well.

When Todd told me to follow the sound of his voice and return to the present, I was still crying. I was curled up in a ball and just wanted to be left alone for a while. It was a heavy thing I had just accomplished.

Although I was so relieved to have that weight off of me, I had still just revisited the trauma center with Nick.

Todd told Larry there was no need to bring me back to a state of full awareness yet. He suggested Larry hold me and let me re-enter the room at my own place, space, and timing. He said the coming days would include more awareness and clarity, and if needed he would help me further.

Larry curled up beside me, and held me until I fell asleep... this time he was with me through it all, holding my hand and he did not let go.

I find that being able to return to a memory with the insights and awareness of the moment is so very precious. As a memory I always have the ability to speak to that situation from a position of knowledge and make appropriate invitations to heal, to grow, and/or make positive change.

That day in trance, my husband watched me come to new terms and heal from a moment which had been a profound, continuing nightmare.

He made a decision to learn more about hypnosis. "If that's what is possible..." he wanted to learn more about it. Phenomenal magic.

From that moment forward I have been free... I have been free.

I have been *free*.

Larry Becomes My Hero

One of the phenomenal things about hypnosis is that at its core the value is to create a path which can lead you through profound healing as well as balance when necessary.

There is no timeline and the invitation is there to make available shifts and changes at your own speed and in your own time. Because of this fact, it is not uncommon for me to have a hypnosis session, then a few hours, days, or even weeks later, another piece of the puzzle falls into perfect position. When one thing is adjusted all the tension that had been accumulated (or in my case, the associated crap) is invited to shift and heal as well.

One of the many tools available for this transition is called "reframing."

You know how different a picture looks when you change its position by displaying it differently or putting it in a different light? Albert Einstein said, "When you look at something differently, what you are looking at changes." This statement has become my truth, so when I face a challenge that seems bigger than I desire to deal with, I seek a way to look at it differently.

I must say at first it took a lot of time and effort but now years later I am pretty good at it.

This is the story of one of my initial WOW moments of reframing.

This story begins about three days after Todd helped me to unlock and heal the deep trauma of the night Nick suffered a massive stroke.

I'd had three days of sorting things out, checking out what was now possible, and wondering if this feeling of a two-ton weight being lifted off my heart was real.

Larry and I were sitting in our hot tub just talking, when all of a sudden I looked at him with a fresh perspective—a new view—and he became my hero.

With all the facts in place, I stopped viewing him as the villain who "let me down" all those years ago by not being there.

On July 15, 1995, in Mannheim, Germany, when our 17-year-old son Nick collapsed at a youth group meeting, the ambulance was called. I had been at a ladies' bible study nearby and someone rushed over to get me when it was apparent that Nick was not okay.

When I arrived he was on the ground. In my peripheral vision, I located my other children, Bryan and Rachel, and went to my knees. I was told he had not been responsive since he had collapsed, and that an ambulance was on the way. To the best of my ability, I was holding my son in my arms while he was dying on the ground.

I shouted for everyone to start praying. I said it with the authority of a mom fighting for her son's life. It was apparent to me that it was absolutely necessary.

Nick opened his eyes for me. I asked where his car keys were (like that mattered!), and he reached into his pocket and flipped them toward me. It was a sign of life. I knew my son was still with us.

The ambulance arrived with a car load of emergency room doctors right behind it. With four doctors on site, it was clear our lives had just exploded.

Nick was transported to the Mannheim Hospital and rushed into the trauma center. I sat with my friend Anne and the shock gave us a short moment of being numb and dumb. I had no idea I was about to lose all veils of being naïve.

A doctor came and said they needed me in the room immediately.

I answered their questions. I told them my son did not do drugs. They agreed this was not a drug-related issue.

They told me Nick was in bad shape, and he needed me. No one else in the room spoke fluent English. He needed the comfort of a language and a voice he understood.

I saw my son on that trauma table in the blinding light. They said he appeared to be paralyzed on his right side and that he had probably suffered a stroke. To say this moment was horrendous is only sufficient because I cannot find a bigger word.

The world around me disappeared. The only thing I focused on was my precious son. He opened his eyes, looked at me, and was terrified, beyond comprehension. The timing between him looking me in the eye and him being on total life support in ICU could not have been more than a few minutes. His life flashed before me. All I could think was, *Oh dear God, please. I am not done being his mom yet.*

The American military community was activated for a full response for our family. Larry's office showed up. Our friends, commanders, and chain of commands went into full protocol to locate Larry in Italy where he was deployed for the Bosnian conflict, and to get him home as soon as possible. He was located smoothly and the process of getting him back to us began.

After they got Nick settled into his bed in ICU, the life support was all hooked up and his care was settled, they allowed me in to see him. I took one look at my first born child, my baby, my son and I lost it. The scream which came out of me must have reverberated throughout the entire world. If you felt the earth shake that night, it would not surprise me. Machines and tubes and medications and his still body just laying there, no response.

I had to be carried out of his room.

Around midnight they determined Nick's condition was beyond the level of "extraordinary measures" to maintain his life. It was decided that the chances of his survival or recovery were slim to none. But it was also determined that since they already had the life support connected there was no need to shut him off before his father arrived, since I had gotten so upset earlier.

Never, ever underestimate the power of a scream.

Through the night and into the next day, Nick was quiet. I held his hand with my heart and prayed for a miracle of magnitude.

One arrived.

At about 4 pm the next afternoon, our community commander's wife, Mary Jo Youngs, burst onto the scene with the commander of the American dispensary. Mary Jo also happened to be the mother of Nick's best friend Raymond. She had heard something happened to Nick. She brought the biggest arsenal at her disposal: an American doctor.

He went into conference with the hospital staff and after a briefing, he asked for extreme measures to save Nick. The Americans would medevac him back to America as soon as possible, so the Germans just needed to sustain life until then.

By American medical standards Nick was not beyond hope, but within the fulcrum of the German socialized medical system his score was too high to maintain.

Two hours of conference calls to Munich, Berlin, Hanover, and Heidelberg ensued to determine what to do for Nick.

Around 6 pm Larry finally made it to the hospital. He had been pretty sure the reports he received were exaggerated and things were not as bad as he had been told. He arrived, wrapped me in his arms, and thought for just a few minutes that his biggest challenge would be calming me down.

That was not the case.

The American doctor called us through the door to the private counseling room and shared the medical staff's recommendation.

Nick was headed into brain surgery to release the pressure in his head. There were no promises but at least it would give him a fighting chance. His brain was swelling. The scans showed a huge clot had exploded in his head and full damage had yet to be determined.

After surgery I took the days, and Larry took the nights so our son was never alone. One week later, Nick was weaned from life support. Our son was still in there.

I was asked to stay out of the room, but as the drugs were reduced, Larry sat and talked to him. "Nick, open your eyes. This is your dad. Squeeze my hand, son. I've got you."

They arm wrestled a bit as Nick's muscles twitched. A tremendous sign! There are no words to express these moments accurately.

Following Nick's awakening, I walked into the room where they had him propped in a special chair. I went to my knees, looked into his eyes, and took his hand. The first word he said to me was a stuttered and hard-fought, "MOM." In all my life I have never heard a sweeter word spoken. I had my son back. Nothing else in the entire world mattered at that moment.

Never underestimate the power of a good scream!

Fast forward... For a decade and a half I had resented Larry for not being there with me during those first 24 hours. I stood that ground alone (which is inaccurate because I was surrounded the entire time). He was not there.

After an agonizing 24 hours, he arrived when the doctors finally had a plan. He heard a message of Nick's potential recovery instead of his imminent death.

I had held Larry accountable somewhere deep inside of me, beyond my thinking ability to forgive. "You weren't there, dammit!"

He took my attitude in stride and assumed it was a fight without teeth. He had no defense because he had not done anything wrong. He got there as soon as he could.

Back at home, three days after my hypnosis session which released the pressure of the trauma room. I was living in a state of almost-freedom that had yet to be defined.

Suddenly I looked at Larry and started to cry. "Thank you," I told him. "Thank you," I continued to sob.

Confusion reigned for a few moments until I got my new thoughts together. In that moment I realized Larry had not abandoned me. *He had actually saved our son's life that day.*

It had taken the Americans 22 hours to show up and demand the machines *not* be shut off. It had taken 24 hours for a plan to be created to allow him a chance to live. And Larry did not arrive until *after* those determinations had been made.

The time it took for him to travel from Italy saved my son. Had he been with me they would have shut off the machines and we would have watched Nick die.

So there I was, thanking Larry for taking so long to get back. He was my hero.

Larry just stared at me, understanding a phenomenal magical shift had just occurred. He had just become my hero. The 'I stood that ground alone' became 'I had the worst day of my life and thank you for not being there.'

After that everything shifted quickly. I was not only willing to heal, I wanted to heal. Strange things came into fresh focus. New perspectives opened up as Subconscious and I cried together, then healed together.

I no longer recognized my life as it had been for so long.

Freedom has a way of doing that for you.

Gateway

During one of my very first experiences in trance, I was introduced to my subconscious through the phenomena of hypnosis. This connection quickly became a friendship. From the moment I met her we developed a working partnership which changed my life.

My subconscious has become my best friend. She fights with me or for me. She provides unconditional love and protection. When I met my subconscious, she began to shift how I see, feel, and experience who I truly am. Her point of view was refreshing, encouraging and something worth the effort.

Before meeting her, I kept people at arm's length. Most did not even realize it. I gave the impression of confidence with strength. Only those closest to me knew the truth. There was much within me I worked hard to keep hidden.

Hello, Subconscious!

She knew me from within. The self-assessment of being hollow vanished.

We all have a Subconscious though most people do not take even five minutes of the day to acknowledge that part of them who holds all their:

1. *Habits*. We did not have to relearn how to get dressed this morning. We did not have to search for our beds last night. Yet every time my family has relocated, during the first week, I would lose my keys, my phone, my purse, my shoes and my glasses more than once. Subconscious now realized I needed to place my things in a similar location each time. She looked at me

and said, "You know what? We are going to create a habit right here, right now." I quit losing things. She saw a pattern develop and instinctively knew it would be best for me to repeat it so my thinking mind would have one less thing to focus upon. *Thank you, Subconscious.*

2. *Emotions.* She knows how we feel and, usually why as well. There is not a requirement to begin laughing today because tomorrow at five o'clock something is going to be funny. Nor is it required to be angry now just in case someone cuts us off in traffic on the way home. Subconscious holds our emotions and is more than able to bring forward the one or more that fit the situation and personality of the moment. Our emotions are personal. What gives one of us nervous anxiety might give someone else a sense of relief. You are unique and Subconscious is more than capable to sort things out for our highest and greatest good. *Thank you, Subconscious.*

3. *Memories.* She holds an enormous repository of our life moments. They are placed inside and organized with an internal time/date/place and point-of-view stamp. If I were to ask you your mom's first name, you probably would be able to bring up information with ease. It might seem like it was just waiting to come forth. But the truth is if I had not asked, you might not have concentrated on her name for quite some time. Our entire life— from the womb to this moment—is kept within her trusted care. *Thank you, Subconscious.*

4. *Imagination.* For me this attribute is the one I most appreciate. Subconscious holds and activates our imagination. That's where the good stuff is. Imaginations are the cooperative components of all we are. She might activate a memory while clarifying a request. Our imagination has the privilege of adding or subtracting at will. Whether I choose to dream either at night,

during the day or for a specific desire, she is ever diligent. *Thank you, Subconscious.*

When I awakened to the powerful presence of my subconscious, I made it my passionate focus to get to know her better… and in doing so, I got to know myself. I love her with the heart of a best friend… and the magic is, she loves me right back.

The peace, calm, and ease are available for us all.

Hypnosis is the gateway I used to begin a fresh way of looking at things. In that process I found "all of me." Hypnosis opened doors previously closed by my limited thinking, allowing me to better evaluate situations. Ever since the new pathways were created, I have maintained a loyalty to the vehicle that got me there.

Be prepared for it to resonate within you as I invite your subconscious to read along. That intimate connection is as close as your next breath.

What Would I Have Missed?

The next section of this book is dedicated to Sondra stories. I welcome you to journey with me into the adventures of a life transformed.

I didn't begin with issues that were of no consequence. I began with health concerns, my marriage, my job, and releasing the pressure of a traumatic event. Once I found something that worked for me I chose to incorporate it fully into my life.

The growing relationship with my subconscious is a lifeline now. It joins the whimsical with the outrageous. We laugh, we cry, we live, and we love.

I could have stopped and said, "Well that was interesting," but I didn't. I stood within the phenomena of being a hypnosis subject and created a life which is richer than anything I might have created without it.

With each new hypnotic experience I think, "Wow, if I had stopped, what would I have missed?"

I don't want to miss anything. I want it all.

A friend recently told me I had no idea what pain feels like because I hadn't been in her shoes. I wanted to say to her, "Well do you want to trade your issues for mine?" But I did not. She is right, I don't know her pain. I have however found the place that works for me to heal from my own.

If I stop now, what will I have missed? I don't want to find out... so I am not stopping.

Welcome to my world.

I want to share with you, as you read my stories, that your intro to hypnosis could be motivated by any number of issues.

My issues were my own, but it could've been anything.

This is merely a collection of my encounters. My challenges are not necessarily yours, and vice versa.

When I say, "It could have been anything," this is my way of encouraging you to consider the depth of healing available to you when you partner with your subconscious. As you read you may see/feel/touch/remember areas of your life that are seeking a similar opportunity to heal. Perhaps these are issues I have not personally experienced, but if you have… then this is for you as well.

I tip my hat to you and suggest you give your subconscious a chance. The voice may come in images or a small whisper, in a manner you can hear aloud, or merely one you can understand.

But ask yourself… "If I'm not willing to give this a try, what will I have missed?"

Go for Phenomenal

What is the difference between living an extraordinary life, an amazing life, or a phenomenal life?

Here is my personal viewpoint.

Living an *extraordinary* life is admirable. At its core is striving to achieve an increase of ordinary things: things everyone has in their day-to-day lives such as electronics, a bigger house, better car, prestigious job or larger bank account. It is a life where you compare what you have to what others possess and feel good about your personal success. It can be competition driven, yet at its core is the belief, "I will have a better life if I have more to show for it."

Living an *amazing* life allows for adventure and exploration. It is living in *a maze*. This maze has twists and turns, it has exciting possibilities of what may be around the next corner. Living an amazing life allows you to dream and believe that there is always more "out there." It also comes with the safety of knowing there are walls surrounding you at all times and some sort of path to be followed. Life in the maze can and will be very exciting as you get out of it what you put into it. It's that treasure hunt, the opportunity to believe in things yet to be seen, and knowing as life continues you can always step forward into "what else is possible."

But this is my favorite and what I strive for:

Living a *phenomenal* life gives you the freedom to know that, "If you walk through that door, everything changes," and then deciding, "I'm going for it!" It is a life where belief systems you've held onto so tightly begin to release and are allowed to be transformed into ways yet to be discovered. Phenomenal living can be accomplished by anyone, anywhere. It has no social structure, no limiting factors. A phenomenal life does not require anything extra. It is simply free of the limitations of the maze. Phenomenal living is the invitation for you right here, right now, to allow your life to be ever expanding.

Phenomenal living is watching the clouds gift you with an image, or walking down the street and allowing a smell to catch your memory. It is looking at turquoise and asking yourself, "Is that blue or green? I always forget." Then you smile.

Within hypnosis, you will continually be challenged to look at what you perceive as belief, and to ask yourself if that specific belief still serves your highest and best interests. If it does not, you and your subconscious can deconstruct, rebuild, then move into a fresh perspective.

The transition into a fresh perspective also means you will no longer keep those past limitations or hold onto blame for your life choices. That can be tough.

My grandson believed he could not roller skate without holding onto the rail or using the kid-cage to keep him upright. His sister took his hand, but no matter what she did or said, he couldn't stay upright until he believed it was possible. For just a moment, he was steady. The light went off in his head. Then he was willing to actually try to skate free. There is nothing more beautiful to observe than a child finding his feet beneath him when the ground is on wheels. He wobbled a bit as his belief system shifted... but then he no longer fell down.

So what does happen when everything changes?

There is really only one way to find out. When the dependency on the things in your life are revealed as no longer necessary, your limitations are free. Boundaries are erased.

Believing is the toughest part.

Sleeping in the Alps

One of the amazing things about hypnosis is that there are so many choices. If one solution turns out to be a less than perfect fit, you can shift and try something else.

As you will learn later, my husband Larry became so fascinated by the possibilities he saw with hypnosis, he pursued training and certification. I had already discovered how much I loved being a hypnosis subject, so it seemed natural to let Larry practice his budding skills with me.

We looked for tools and topics to try together.

One concept we hoped to reinforce through hypnosis was the power of *habit*. If you can do something consistently for 21-30 days… if you focus on that task intentionally, it can become a subconscious habit. You can then move on with your life, comfortably allowing that habit to just flow without any further effort.

We also wanted to practice (we often call it "play"). The technique of *direct suggestion* was a great place to start. In this tool, Larry would verbally lead trance time while I listened and simply followed his suggestions for my benefit. Some might call this a guided journey… with no pressure!

Additionally, we learned hypnosis can be used to address sleep challenges, either for the person who cannot go to sleep, or who once asleep has trouble staying that way. For me, it was the latter, so we decided to combine these three concepts and tools for our next practice session.

I would normally wake up several times a night. To imagine hypnosis could give me the freedom to get a better night's rest was amazing. To imagine it could be provided through a tranquil and relaxing session was even better. *How cool! I'm about to be given another opportunity to go to sleep!*

In our experience, we found that suggestions (especially those which include imaginary environments created in the session) tended to resemble things I have seen or experienced before. The memory banks of my mind go to something known rather than creating everything from scratch. For me, it is quite common to find I've included a snapshot from a movie, TV show, or past experience. I also discovered that I experience trance time, and the words of my guide very literally.

This session brought back images from the movie *The Edge* and a junior high youth group trip taken with my kids to the JungFrau in Switzerland years ago.

For comfort, we laid down on our bed together. Our intentions were set to create a successful hypnosis session to help me stay asleep through the night (or at least reduce the number of times I would wake).

Larry suggested I was at the base of a beautiful mountain. I immediately pictured myself in Switzerland, at the base of the Jungfrau, looking at the mountain streams and meadow flowers in the shadow of snowy mountain peaks. A waterfall in the distance provided a vista unlike any I've experienced before or since. I recognized this place and it was both comforting and relaxing.

My husband was there beside me and invited me to take a walk with him.

We enjoyed the peace-filled scenic stroll. He said he was going to lead me through the valley. My thinking mind said there was no valley between the mountains at Jungfrau, but it also knew Larry had no idea where my hypnotic journey had taken me. My subconscious knew to let the detail slide. "Silly man," I thought. "These are BIG mountains. You can't walk between them!"

Magically however, my imagination transported me to a gorgeous valley. We stepped through and he pointed out a still and beautiful crystal clear lake. A huge log chalet sat within the trees at the water's edge.

My imagination took me to the hunting lodge from the movie *The Edge*. He suggested that since we had been walking for a long time we should sit and relax, to breathe in the cool mountain air and share a blanket for a few minutes. "Yummy!" I think we may have watched the sun set and the moon rise.

Are you starting to see why I love hypnosis so much?

If the session had ended right there, I would have been completely happy. But our glorious experience continued.

Larry told me to turn and walk up the steps to the front door of the lodge. With each step I would realize how tired I was, that it had been a wonderful day, and how good it was going to feel to lay down and get a full night's sleep.

He suggested I go to the front desk and pick up my room key. I was surprised when the desk clerk knew my name and welcomed me back. He told me my room was, "Up those stairs, third door on the left."

Again with each step I realized how much my great day was ready to be finished by laying down for a wonderful night's sleep.

The key fit perfectly, the door swung open and I stepped into an amazingly comforting room. The bed was made from strong wood, and the linens and curtains were all white. But the balcony view… breathtaking! Moonlight on the water glistened up onto my balcony and beckoned me to come out and see more.

Larry began to describe the items on the balcony. I had a small table with two chairs, a firm railing to lean against, and in the corner were three stones. I imagined them as medium to large decorative rocks. I stepped up to the railing looking at the moon, relaxed and feeling as if I was floating. There was nothing more to do than just let the moment absorb into me.

Next Larry suggested I pick up the first stone and toss it into the lake, like skipping a rock across the surface of the still calm waters. I thought, *Crap, I can barely lift that thing.* So I struggled to pick it up and somehow plopped it over the railing where it rolled into the water. There was no splash, but it wasn't graceful either.

He suggested that as I took the second stone I would realize I felt even more tired. *No shit*, I thought, *these rocks are heavy.* The second one was a bit smaller and at least it made it into the water. Same with the third… his soft voice suggested I was so tired I could barely throw the final remaining stone.

He was right. I released that rock as fast as I could and was glad when he told me to walk back inside and sit down on the bed.

Larry settled me into the covers, fluffed my pillow, and gave me the most tender kiss. My husband told me he loved me dearly and that this night would hold me in slumber until I awoke fresh and clear the next morning. The night did not require my attention, he said. It was not only okay, but suggested, that I allow the night to proceed without me.

After the session we had fun laughing about Jungfrau, the movie's hunting lodge, and especially the big heavy rocks. We agreed to repeat this trance plan for the next few nights to see if it would assist me in forming a sleep-all-night habit.

The next night the rocks were much smaller. Within a week, I had added a small table to my balcony and the stones were smooth in my hand, not heavy. I became good at skipping stones, able to skim them for several jumps across the water.

As expected, with the intention for success and the repeated suggestions, I began to sleep through the night. Together we created a habit of better sleep. I loved my mountain lake, cool breeze, moonlit balcony and that exquisite bedroom. It was working!

One evening weeks later, we had a chance to go back to our mountain retreat. By now it was rote in my mind. I knew what Larry was going to say. Following his instructions was easy.

That evening I got my keys and followed his words... followed them *exactly*. When I woke the next morning I told him he had made me break a couple of windshields last night. He looked perplexed. "Honey," I told him, "my room is up the stairs and third door on the *left*. You sent me to the third one on the *right*. When I tossed the stones off my balcony, it hit the cars in the parking lot."

It's amazing how literal our minds can be. In trance, we are willing to accept suggestions by someone we trust... and I trust my husband implicitly... much to the detriment of a red VW Bug and a black Saab.

The purpose of this trance work was to assist me to sleep better through the night. I no longer randomly wake. The only times I wake now are when I need to pee! Mission accomplished. What's next?

Weight Loss

Weight Loss is a Journey

Throughout much of adult life, my weight has been steady and quite stable. I stayed at the same shape and size for many years. In the blink of an eye though, all that shattered after my son Nick suffered a massive stroke at age 17.

His life rested in God's hands, and by His grace Nick lived. Yet in that moment, my life shifted from that of a multitasking Army wife who would do anything for anyone, to someone focused on becoming an absolute healing machine with 1000% effort dedicated to my own family.

Within months, my weight crept past 200 pounds, and although I knew it, I could not have cared less.

I remember looking at my good friend in her size 20 jeans thinking how large her backside looked in those big pants. Yet when it was my body in the size 20 pants I just kept expanding with ease.

In that same blink of an eye our family finances tanked. As a soldier family stationed in Germany, Nick's medical bills were covered, but other expenses such as gas to attend rehab, items for his recovery, and the needs of my other two kids (who needed pocket money while they stayed with whomever could take care of them while I helped Nick) were not.

Where could I choose to cut corners to meet our financial needs?

Facing growing credit debt, I turned to the kitchen and homemade foods as a cost-saving measure. I "paid" with my time, making cheap yet delicious homebaked bread. I could create the dough with my love and attention, and the product was very filling.

I made a fresh loaf almost every night for supper. Sundays were extra special: donut night!

My life revolved around getting us through the days and into the nights. The work although exhausting was filled with little things that make living a blessing. In June 1996 Nick stood with Mannheim High School at the Dom in Worms, Germany, as a graduating senior. This is the same cathedral where Martin Luther took his stand against the powerful forces of his day, saying boldly, "Here I stand. I cannot do otherwise. God, help me."

As they called his name, Nick stepped forward and took his diploma in one hand, then hugged his vice principal with both arms and his whole heart. Beside me in the crowd, his sister rose to her feet. Within seconds the entire crowd was standing, cheering and crying all at the same time. Nick had done it. He had survived. He had thrived, and there he stood— tall, strong, and oh my God, so *alive!*

I stood cheering my son in my size 20 dress knowing that every minute, every mile, every step, and every prayer had been worth whatever it took to get him there.

Our family was soon on its way to a new duty assignment in Annapolis, Maryland. This also allowed us to be close to Walter Reed Army Medical Center for Nick's continued health care and recovery needs.

Moving three Army-raised teenagers onto a naval base is not for the weak of heart. On the first morning after our trans-Atlantic flight, we pulled onto base housing and almost in unison, the three complained that there were no tanks, only anchors. I fixed their despair with a huge McDonald's breakfast—which none of us had enjoyed in more than three years.

We spent the next year taking necessary steps to allow Nick to move into his adult life with the best possible potential. Just two years to the day after he collapsed, he got on a plane bound for Texas and a job corps facility.

My 24/7 mom-on-a-mission marathon took a breath. Almost immediately my health began to deteriorate.

I was diagnosed with severe acid reflux, which had destroyed the base of my esophagus. I was given two options: live on prescription meds for the rest of my life, or go in for surgical repair.

After the years we had just plowed through it was an easy decision. I wanted to fix it!

I was more surprised than embarrassed when the surgical nurse had to cut my wedding ring off my hand. It had become too tight to remove otherwise.

She very sweetly talked to me while her little ring cutter freed my trapped finger.

The recovery was tougher than I anticipated, possibly because I was just tired. This gave my mind and body time to slow down. The timing of my surgery was very close to Larry's Army retirement and moving into our new home. It meant switching to another new school for my two younger kids—high school, at that.

I was so focused on the needs of my family that I had established no close friends. Instead I gave my time, efforts, and need to be a caregiver to my yard and gardens.

Although that was fun, it didn't include much exercise, nor was I ever more than a moment away from my kitchen. The fact that I am an excellent cook didn't help. And now I could eat anything I wanted since my esophagus was healed.

Larry replaced my wedding ring with another that fit my enlarged hand size.

Weeks faded to months, months to years. We lived, we loved, we raised our kids, and we savored every day. I had a great life. Laughter was a constant. We rebuilt our lives, post-stroke and post-Army with few regrets. We made good friends and had tons of fun knowing that living in the present moment felt the best it had ever been.

Until it got even better.

My husband and I decided to go on another cruise vacation. The first one had been fantastic. For the next one we'd travel with our best friends. We planned and paid for it for more than a year. When it came time to buy clothes for the trip I had to find a local "Big Gals" shop. I bought beautiful stuff off the last season sale rack, enjoying the fact there were so many nice things in size 22/24-2/3X

I should have been wearing size 26 but instead I just added an extra X to my purchase, and cut off the tags as soon as they came into the house. It was okay if they were just a bit tight. They fit.

I got on that ship weighing 270 pounds. The seat belt on the airplane had been too tight, and sharing a seat in a row of three had me crammed up against the window.

As a person I was happy, my life was awesome, and weight seemed to have no bearing on the quality of my personal identity. That was… until I refused to go to dinner with our friends because for the first time in my life I felt ugly.

Most of the cruise was fun: relaxing by the solarium pool, dinners in the main dining room, watching the sunset over the ocean. Life was very, very good. But then came formal night. This was the moment when I came face to face with the woman in the mirror for the first time in years.

What I saw crushed me.

I put on my formal dress, stepped in front of the full-length mirror and lost my ability to breathe.

The dress, although beautiful, was not beautiful on me. I saw a fat woman looking back at me for the first time in my life. I ripped it off my body, threw it on the floor and refused to go to the main dining room. Larry and our friends tried to understand how the happy-go-lucky, always smiling, always jolly Sondra had crashed so hard so fast.

They had not seen me in the dress!

This was a pivotal moment in my life. After I quit crying I went out on the top deck of the ship to take in some night air. I had no idea how significant that night would be for my future path.

Not too long after returning home, we realized hypnosis had tools and processes which could assist weight loss. I knew that if it was possible, I wanted to try it.

My daughter Rachel had taken a job as executive producer with ABC Baltimore. I told her I was going to try Sheila Granger's *Virtual Gastric Lapband*[©] hypnotic protocol. Without mentioning my name or situation, she called her news director and suggested it might be a fun news story.

The news director just happened to phone my hypnotist and asked to follow the progress of a client. The hypnotist called me and asked if a news crew could come and film our sessions. A few days later I was being interviewed and filmed during my initial Gastric Lapband session.

The story was a big hit and I represented hypnosis well. I was a large lady many could relate to. When asked why I was interested in losing weight, I told my story of gradually growing to be 270 pounds with little to no concern about it. I explained this would be my first ever weight loss journey. I had no yo-yo habits and felt like a clean slate for positive change.

The weight loss via hypnotic assistance was profound. My mind and body were in agreement to respond as if I'd had the physical surgery. We co-created the protocol with eating and exercise in my agreement. I was able to follow the simple instructions, and the weight started to reduce.

I listened to audio recordings, not only of the Virtual Gastric Lapband protocol but also those of other brilliant hypnotists. During my fifteen-minute breaks at work, I'd sit in my car and absorb the messages with my subconscious.

I started going to the gym every day. Progress happened, the weight was coming off. My muscles were getting toned and my desire to be an example for the power of hypnosis was shining. Everyone knew what I was doing because my story had been on TV.

My clothing sizes dropped rapidly. The news crew returned to our home when I weighed 242. I was so excited... that was nearly 30 pounds gone!

It was a powerful incentive.

My weight and improved health habits continued until I got stuck at 218 pounds. Now I realize that 218 is a helluva lot better than 270, but the scale had quit moving.

Not understanding why, I accepted the moment as a victory. In the after-glow of that accomplishment though, my focus faded. Over the next couple of years the weight began to climb. By spring a couple of years later I was up around 240 pounds again.

Then another of those life changing events happened. We will call this one "Up in Smoke"

In the blink of an eye, a smoldering cigarette was responsible for our house burning down, and the only clothes I owned were the ones on my back. Details around this event, and the benefits achieved through hypnosis will come out later in my story, but at this one moment in time, what I really needed was a new dress to wear to work.

I found some great spring dresses in size 20-2X. After watching everything we owned go up in an inferno, *any* new dress (regardless of size) felt pretty damn good. I rebuilt a simple wardrobe of versatile items. With help from insurance, we settled into a rental home and life crept forward.

Then one evening in July I took a step, just like any other. My knee gave way and the pain was excruciating. I could neither stand nor walk, and I was sure that nothing had ever hurt that bad before.

Larry came to my side immediately with direct suggestion hypnosis. We have become skilled at including hypnosis in our day-to-day lives, and because it was a habit, there was no hesitation for hypno to be the front line tool in this crisis. It helped tremendously.

I was a 55-year-old, 242-pound woman with a torn meniscus.

September brought me to a surgical center for knee repair. I had decided the pain had been so awful that post-surgical recovery could not possibly hurt as bad. That probably would have been true if the knee had not been filled with arthritis. With post-surgical swelling, and despite therapy and following medical advice, the pain was better but not yet tolerable. And certainly not gone.

I returned to the surgeon in November to be told I had really bad knees. The recovery was being delayed by the arthritis. Most importantly, the doctor said there was no way my knees would age with me at that shape and size.

My mother and father had both had left and right knees replaced. I was not even remotely interested in knee replacement, then or in the future.

The spring dresses I bought after the fire were not going to be warm enough for the winter. I needed to make a decision and get serious about losing significant weight—for my knees, my wallet, and my wardrobe, as well as my health.

I chose to talk with a friend who is an Optimal Health life-coach focused on building habits for positive living through safe and healthy weight loss. She explained a plan for someone like me, who needed to lose significant weight but could not aggressively exercise.

There I was, 100 pounds overweight and unable to walk more than ten minutes.

I spoke with her about my absolute commitment to the magic of hypnosis. She was not only on board, but felt it would complement her life-coaching program beautifully. Optimal health for life was an element I had never embraced. I had taken my health, my body and my weight for granted. It was time to take a positive step to make the change.

Through my entire adult life I have avoided mirrors. I find fault with my self-image and it is much easier to just brush my teeth and hair, give mirror-me a smile and get on with my day.

I feel the same about cameras. I delete or refuse to look at most pictures of me more than once. I love me—I do not like to upset myself intentionally.

In four months, I dropped from 242 to 207 pounds and looked healthier than ever before. One day a friend clicked a picture of me… I had *no idea* how much different I looked! When I saw that picture, I thought, *Who is that woman? OMG, is that me??*

The weight-loss transformation was profound. Hypnosis gave me the courage to face and accomplish the tough stuff, have hard conversations with myself, and to fully rejoice in the journey.

Lose 90 Pounds Instantly

I have an ultimate weight goal to be as healthy as possible. I am not interested in fad solutions. I will stick with what I know works… and this has worked for me.

Once I made the decision to reduce my weight partnered with hypnosis, it got fun. My subconscious and I began to create choices and see possibilities from the first moment.

Hypnosis, at its core, is a tool for positive change. It invites us, mind, body and spirit, to join together. The one thing all of "us" have in common is imagination. My subconscious is the keeper and activator of those shared imaginations. She assists in acting them out, and let's face it, if it can be imagined, you can have a relationship with it.

There are many brilliant hypnotists out there—each with a different personality and perspective. I have worked with several in person, or through their audio recordings, to instill my new habits and routines in my life.

One such suggestion was to open my imagination and create an image of how I desired to look. Even though the hypnotist suggested a mental picture, I desired something more.

I normally cringe to have my picture taken, but because I had an earnest desire for positive change, I invited my daughter Rachel to the house. In our front yard stands a magnolia tree. That poor thing has rebounded through many tough winters, so I chose it for the spot to make my stand and have my picture taken—all of me—straight on.

In the industry this is known as my "before" picture.

Then my daughter was photographed in the exact same spot. I consider her to be one of the most beautiful women I've ever met. I outweighed her by at least 90 pounds on that day.

We went back in the house and uploaded the pictures to a photo-editing software. In just a few minutes, we swapped my head onto Rachel's shoulders. With a bit of photo-magic, there I stood in the image, a picture of me at a reduced weight... a picture I could approve of, and appreciate... a picture in which I could rejoice.

My head on the body of my daughter, the vision of my goal self came into reality.

I was beautiful.

A funny neckline "scar" was the only evidence it was a photoshopped pic.

Now I had a visual image of myself 90 pounds lighter. The change occurred instantaneously. I showed the new creation to my husband, and he was so proud of the concept, he made copies and hung them next to my bathroom mirror and bed frame so I could look at them, be reminded of my goal, and know the path offered to me each day.

It is hard to describe how it felt to see myself, literally in my daughter's shoes. It allowed me to see myself as beautiful when I looked at this picture of "us."

When Rachel offered to help me in any way with this weight loss journey, I'm sure she didn't expect me to ask to share her body! But then again she wasn't surprised when her mom came up with an outrageous solution for such a complex personal issue.

In truth, it was a piece of copy paper, run through our home printer. A silly game of a mother and daughter combining pictures of themselves for a shared goal. Or was it more?

When the hypnotist asked me to create a mental image of my ideal self, and then identify with that new "me," it was hard. But looking into my eyes atop my daughter's slim figure in that doctored selfie, the goal became so much more tangible.

More than my heart would become lighter.

Do you ever wonder what you would look like at your ideal shape and size? If so, find a friend or a family member—or even a picture on the internet. Do a little photo editing and *see* what's possible when you allow yourself to partner with *your* imagination.

Weight Loss to Weightless

The size and shape of my body was reducing. Everyone around me noticed and watched my progress. I was dedicated to success and it showed. It felt good to be treating my mind and body with equal respect, knowing that through the magic of hypnosis they had been partnered perfectly.

But I needed to find more joy in the journey. I needed a reward.

As long as I kept it fun I could keep it going. Keeping it fun was one of the components that Subconscious and I worked together to achieve continually.

So we made an agreement: I would notice sights, sounds, and the happenings surrounding me with greater clarity. The intention of this game was to sharpen my ability to pick up on the subtle fun surrounding me. Sometimes it would be something whimsical. Other times it would be a license plate or a shared conversation with a perfect message. I grinned, I giggled, and the weight kept reducing.

But I wanted more. I decided that when I got to the halfway point of my weight loss goal—220 pounds—we would celebrate. It had to be something I could not have done before. Something that was now possible because of my weight loss… something perfectly outrageous…

Skydiving!

I asked my daughter Rachel if she would join me on jump day. Of course she said, "Yes!"

We both told Larry it would be a celebration and we wanted the works: the dive, the photos, and the video. *I wanted it ALL.*

With that goal set in motion I continued to create a mind and body that met skydiving standards. I did my research and the nearest site restricted to a 220-pound weight maximum—which perfectly matched my halfway point. *Game on!*

The day arrived for the big jump. We got up early, forgot the sunscreen and headed for the sky. My celebration momentum was flying high.

We arrived, and realized that due to their schedule we would have a three-hour wait for our turn. Larry, Rachel, and I spent the afternoon laughing, just being family.

But when it was finally our turn… the tandem team decided I was too heavy.

They could have said something while we had sat in the hanger most of the day, but no… they waited until it was my turn… then *turned me down!*

Larry was livid. I met all of their posted requirements easily. The issue, we were told was my height-to-weight ratio. My body size was the problem, not the number on the scale. *Damn it, man!*

We sent Rachel up and watched her take her dive. She was magnificent… and I cried from the ground.

As you may imagine, this was not something my husband was going to let slide. He spoke with the manager and got the name of another skydiving place in New Jersey that used bigger planes with a walk-out jump platform, instead of the tuck and roll method this field used.

Larry called them privately, made a reservation for the next day, then came and sat down next to me.

I was trying hard not to cry. He looked into my eyes and said, "Honey, you are going skydiving tomorrow."

I just shook my head no, as if he had not been paying attention the past few moments.

My beloved explained that he had just created another opportunity and was assured the issues of today would not be repeated.

I was relieved. The only question which remained was, "Rachel, will you go with me?" Fearless, she said yes to her second jump in two days.

The next morning was not as hot, and a beautiful clear day filled with renewed anticipation. Wonderful clouds in the sky. Excitement was in the air, and soon I would be, too.

The new facility was aware what happened to me the day before and kept encouraging me that my weight-loss-celebration dive was going to be the best ever. They joined me in my joy.

This plane was huge. It held at least 25 people. Rachel and I each had our tandem diver, and a photo/video jumper with us. They were an international team with hearts of gold, who obviously loved life and were willing to share their world for our benefit.

My photographer told me that when we got into the air he was going to invite me to dance. When he reached out his hand for me, I would take it and he would twirl me around the sky.

We were positioned in the plane so that I went before Rachel. I had a desire for her to watch me fly. She would be right behind me.

Our jump altitude was reached and the plane began to empty. I felt a mixture of excitement and exuberant joy. Thru hypnosis Larry and I had asked for anything less than joy to stay on the ground.

Before jumping, I turned to look Rachel in the eye. She gave me the thumbs up while I slid over to the open door. I held on as instructed, looked out into the open sky, the earth below unseen.

Rachel would later tell me, "Mom, one second you were there and then… you weren't."

What happened next was the most exhilarating feeling of my entire life. I experienced the joy of flight. *I was flying!* The air around me was spectacular.

The sensation of being weightless was the perfect way to celebrate personal weight loss.

And then, the dance! My photographer reached out for me. I twirled around in pure bliss. I was living my dream. That moment in time will forever be etched in the deepest places within me. I could have stayed there all day.

Even though I couldn't feel any change in altitude, we were reaching the point where the ground was visible. Our open-air flight needed to end. Safety first.

The parachute cord was pulled and suddenly I was jerked hard. The slow return to the ground began. As we came over the top of the hanger my tandem jumper told me to lift my legs to 90-degrees and he was going to slide me onto the ground on my bottom.

Perfect landing accomplished!

Rachel and my photographer had landed before me. He was able to capture pictures of my return to earth as Rachel cheered her mom. I could see Rachel's pride and awe in her dazzling eyes that day.

Standing was a bit of a challenge. It took very little time to realize I was a touch nauseous. My body was adjusting as fast as she could. Let's face it, I'd given her quite a new experience.

Rachel and I slowly walked back to the hanger to see Larry smiling from ear to ear. He had given us the opportunity of a lifetime. And he knew it.

It did not take more than a few minutes to finish our business and walk to the car. By that point, I was seriously not feeling well. My head, my stomach, and my balance were all struggling. Luckily, the excitement and adrenaline had not yet worn off.

I got in the car, and Larry turned on the air conditioning. I asked if I could rest a while before he started driving. That's when things got interesting.

I felt lousy physically, yet I was still on a high unlike anything I can describe with mere words. Larry took care of that smoothly and easily.

He dropped me into trance and called out my subconscious. What moments before had been, "Oh, please don't move the car," became a babbling, bubbly over-the-top chatterbox.

My subconscious started gushing out the joy of flight, telling him how great it was. She was unstoppable with expressions of accomplishment. On a scale of 1 to 10 she was at least a 12.

At one point she said, "Sondra thinks she's going to puke. It's okay, though. She will be fine."

She just kept telling Larry and Rachel with overly dramatic words and motions the experience of absolute freedom.

Larry is not only the best husband in the world, but he's a powerful hypnotist. He realized the significant source of power being created. He simply said, "Subconscious, I need you to anchor this joy of flight into your core for Sondra."

He worked with her hypnotically for a few minutes to grab all the good stuff, and store it in all the right places. He knew that the significance of me recognizing true freedom was something that would be appreciated for more than just that present moment.

I had set a weight-loss goal with a reward of skydiving.

Yet, when I reached it, when I had done everything required, I was still told, "No."

If that first day had been the beginning and end, I would not have been in New Jersey dancing in the sky the next. My subconscious was neither overwhelmed nor deterred by the change in our schedule. She and I processed first with disappointment, then outrageous joy.

Since that day, I can and do fly within my mind. Victoriously!

I feel the lift of the air beneath me and I soar. From the perspective of someone on the ground, I understand I was falling at a tremendous rate, yet it was anything but that for me. I did not feel the *fall*.

I felt only the air current holding me up.

And I still do.

Bit in the Butt

You know how sometimes you get all excited about something... and forget to read the directions?

That moment when you surge forward without first learning the basics, and it bites you in the butt?

Well I am sometimes quite energetic and fail to make sure I have everything I need to know within my knowledge base before proceeding.

Welcome to the life of Sondra!

I was living and breathing my highly successful hypnotic weight loss program. Over the course of a year my weight had been reduced 50 pounds from a high of 270. It was phenomenal and for the most part I was motivated toward success.

One of my practices was dedicated time at our local Planet Fitness. I went to the gym daily and spent about 45 minutes working on various machines and weights, watching my success in inches as well as pounds.

However... I'm sure you see the train wreck ahead. I did not take the time to learn how to use all the machines properly, nor the correct body posture or weight limits. I just did what I saw everyone else doing. I figured the effort would have its own payoff.

It was not too long until I started to feel a bit uncomfortable while working out. "No pain, no gain," I told myself and continued to be what I considered "highly successful" while also feeling more and more out of balance.

I had chosen a mantra of ignorance that essentially said, "Push yourself, and hope for the best."

By the time I chose to listen to my body, I had really damaged my piriformis muscle. In laymen's terms that means I messed up my right butt cheek.

Yes, exercising became a true pain in my ass.

Even worse, the right butt muscle is connected to the right knee. So now my knee and my butt were both in distress. The doctor applauded my dedication to the cause, but scolded me for not stopping before I injured myself.

I went to physical therapy for my knee and butt, while trying to continue to work out for the good of my weight loss intentions.

After some downtime, I was back up to regular workouts at the gym again. It was pretty darn clear that ignorance was *not* bliss.

Larry sent me to the gym with a specific assignment. I was to find a trainer and have him coach me on just five machines. I would learn how to use each of those machines perfectly: the correct height of the chair for my body, the positioning, the proper movement, speed of motion and appropriate weight for my current body shape, size, and general abilities.

As he sent me out for my research project, Larry activated my imagination and subconscious to go as partners.

I spent an hour at the gym and learned how to properly use five of the machines I had been playing on for months. The trainer looked at my body position and made subtle adjustments to my form and scope of exercise. I had already established a relationship with this gym equipment, so it was amazing to see how many little tweaks were necessary to shift the machine and its use for my ultimate good.

I came back home ready for a fresh start using tools which were already familiar.

Larry and I settled into a quiet spot for some directed trance time. He settled me into a comfortable trance then called out Subconscious (whom we had named Intuition), and also the part of me that is most dedicated to paying close attention to my shape and size (which we named Image).

Intuition and Image came forward for a chat. They both agreed that I now had a clear knowledge of how to work the machines, how to hold my body and the scope of the intention of the exercise.

Image, Intuition, and I then followed Larry's simple instructions to step into a mental gym of our choosing—one which held all of our newly balanced machines. This mind gym was spectacular. It was bright and soaked in encouragement.

He told us to sit down at the first weighted machine, to settle in and start working with gusto. It was smooth and easy and it felt right. There was no inappropriate movement or strain.

Larry smiled and said, "Okay, keep working, don't stop. You will not get tired from exercising in this gym."

Another machine awaited. Without leaving the first machine, we repeated the drill of working out, with each motion performed thoughtfully and intentionally on the second device. Within a few minutes I had all five machines working simultaneously. It was surreal to watch myself working hard in five different locations at the same time… all of them in sync, all of them working smoothly.

Larry made a suggestion to take me into my mind gym on frequent occasions. We would accomplish hundreds of reps a day, building skill and confidence on the machines during each mind workout. Within a week, when I entered my local gym I did so with confidence and full workout speed and agility.

This tool is called *infinite rehearsal.* We had learned that it was something the Soviets used to do with their MiG pilots to keep them sharp and their skills at expert level without burning precious jet fuel.

As I knew from my post-skydiving nausea, I could not fly a fighter jet… but I could kick butt at the gym.

My recovery took more than a doctor's visit and two months in physical therapy. I had to relearn how to use the gym machines correctly, then build a habit of excellence. As you might expect, after getting back in the gym and perfecting my form with the initial set of five machines, I went back and picked a few more. Larry set the same intention hypnotically for me, and Image was thrilled to have his assistance and the knowledge that she could push me without fear. She now knew I was on a solid foundation to perform better.

Infinite rehearsal gave us the opportunity to realize that *practice* does not make *perfect*. When I was practicing wrong, perfection was not my result. What I need to learn instead was how to *practice perfectly*.

It's a subtle difference, but one my butt appreciates very much.

Gotta Love a Good Mantra

Through the years of being an avid hypnosis subject, I have had the opportunity to meet several amazing hypnotists and have been entranced by many of them. It is interesting how noticeably different the same technique, tool, or suggestion can work under someone else's employ.

It did not take me long to choose to become a Certified Hypnotist myself. Then I was able to not only share from my point of view but I could also take what I had learned through numerous others and make it my own.

Sondra's style of hypnosis is quite unique—as it should be. As a subject and also as a hypnotist I am visual. I can see what is spoken to me in full color images—a video quality scene being played out within me. I can also hear sounds around me and can add textures, sensations. It is this that I bring forward to others as I tell a story or lead a hypnotic session.

If I communicate my experience, then others can enjoy it too. I'll share many more of those stories later, but for now, I want to take you deeper on my hypnotic-assisted weight loss journey.

As with every other professional, continuing education credits are required each year. The field of choices is vast. Everyone out there has a tool, technique, or concept to share with others. This is how and why I came to meet Robert Otto.

I discovered a hypnosis training being taught for a weight-loss program that had been powerful for over 20 years—with thousands of success stories across the country. I already had a sharp interest in hypnotic weight loss so I saw this as an opportunity to learn more about two things that already fit comfortably together for me.

For two days Robert Otto shared his "Fat Ban®" course, and what had worked for his clients under his guidance. He had spent much of the past 20 years traveling the country and filling theaters, auditoriums and gyms with his message: "Keep it simple, be willing to give yourself 30 days to create a new positive habit. Believe in yourself and come back to see me when I return to your city next time… and bring a friend with you."

Without guile or monetary motivation, he invited his audience to return at no additional charge. This gave Robert the chance to see his participants' weight reductions over an extended period of time. He could also enjoy hearing success stories on a personal level, repeatedly.

One of the key components of his "Fat Ban" program is the creation of habit through repetition, to move the task to a subconscious level. Anything repeated for 21-30 days becomes a subconscious habit. (Remember this, because if you choose to create a new habit, you now have the blueprint to follow. Repeat it A LOT. However, if you are doing something daily which you *do not* want to become a habit… you need to stop doing it!)

One of the tools Robert shared is a statement: "I am now in the process of becoming thinner and thinner." It is a simple statement that, when placed within the care of our subconscious, is extremely powerful.

I not only took his class, but when Robert was making an audio recording (for the purpose of sharing with clients remotely), I was the hypnotic subject in his chair. So I learned his program and could also benefit from being a subject as well.

I returned, having made a few friends, and with a deep respect for Robert Otto, who spent his professional life making hypnosis available… and *real* to all who were interested.

He provided a wonderful role model for me. As a hypnotherapist, I want to allow hypno to flow through me in such a way that it is normal and natural for all who work with me. *That's* what I want to do!

I took his "I am now in the process of becoming thinner and thinner" statement home and made it my own. I was determined to create a new habit of weight loss. The instructions were simple: I should repeat this statement for 21-30 days and accept it as a new habit… and acknowledge the truth of those words.

As I took my morning walks this statement transformed beautifully. I could shift my focus between words and phrases, and although repeating the same sentence, I could dramatically influence my intentions.

This became my new mantra:

Statement in full: "I am now in the process of becoming thinner and thinner."

1st lap: *"I"*—me, this is mine, I own this. This is my decision. "I am in the process of becoming thinner and thinner."

2nd lap: *"I AM"*—I am doing this, this is happening now, and right here… right now… I AM. "I AM now in the process of becoming thinner and thinner."

3rd lap: *"I am NOW"*—this is my now, it is something being shifted and changed in this present moment. Right NOW… "I am NOW in the process of becoming thinner and thinner."

4th lap: I am now *"IN THE PROCESS"*—this is a process, I have a responsibility to follow these simple instructions, the process is working for me. I step into this process fully and completely. "I am now IN THE PROCESS of becoming thinner and thinner."

5th lap: I am now in the process *"OF BECOMING"*—This is who I am becoming, the change is happening, the transitions are evident by my personal attitude, choices and newly forming habits. I am becoming. "I am now in the process OF BECOMING thinner and thinner."

6th lap: I am now in the process of becoming *"THINNER AND THINNER"*—the weight reduction is successful within me, my body shape and size are being transformed. I actually am becoming thinner and thinner. "I am now in the process of becoming THINNER AND THINNER."

Robert's statement has another sweet twist. Once the belief has been firmly established within you, it's okay to shorten it. You can allow a fresh, shorter phrase to invoke the same level of habit-forming commitment.

For him, "I am now in the process of becoming thinner and thinner," became simply "Orange Blossom."

Once established firmly within the subconscious, the words "Orange Blossom" would hold equal value to the larger statement as a whole. If you ever see one of his business cards with the statement on one side… and an orange blossom on the other… you'll understand the powerful suggestions being gifted to you.

Because I chose to modify his statement into a six-part journey, I did not ever personally shift over to "Orange Blossom." Yet it is a powerful possibility to allow ourselves to shift focus from one set of words to another and maintain a stream of hypnotic assistance.

This became my personal mantra as I walked, exercised and continued to build a fresh habit for my well-being.

"I am now in the process of becoming thinner and thinner" was my first exposure to building habits intentionally through words I spoke to, and within, myself. I felt in control of the timing, the frequency and the effects that allowed the statement to build within me.

Yes, I was still following someone else's suggestions, but this time I truly understood I was the one creating positive change within myself. For me. *By me.*

Running and Chasing Cows

After I had lost 50 pounds, skydived, and spent countless hours in the local gym, Larry and I realized that regardless of the motivation I cannot... I do not... I will not *run*.

We discussed this at length and decided that my inability and unwillingness to run must have a deep core connection. We both knew that hypnosis and my curiosity would help us discover the reason why. What happened next was both funny and scary at the same time.

Using a tool called *regression to cause*, Larry invited my subconscious to partner in a journey back to the time, place, and space where I first had an "issue" with running. We hoped to locate that moment when I decided that running was a choice, and I ultimately had chosen *no!*

The magic of hypnotic regression is its speed and accuracy at locating pivotal moments no longer stored in active memory. With Larry as my guide, I could listen to his voice and follow his simple instructions. *Game on!* It was now his job to be my escort and ask all the right questions. It was my job to go on the journey.

In very simple terms, Larry asked my subconscious to take me to the first time I ever refused to run.

I was instantly transported back to being a young girl on our family farm outside of Cutler, Indiana, where my dad raised hogs, cattle, and sheep, and grew corn, wheat, and soybeans. The lane back to our barns was about three-quarters of a mile long. Most of the livestock were either penned or grazing within the fields over the hill.

I cannot tell you how often hogs or cattle would find their way out of the fenced area… and have to be chased and herded back into the appropriate place and space.

As a small child it was so scary to be the one trying to make sure they turned in the right direction. We called it "chasing cows." (I am well aware that a "cow" is the mama, but we used the word liberally.)

On our farm, it was the job of the smaller members of the family to stand in the gate or driveway while the older members did the harder work of chasing, turning, and collecting a scattered herd.

Then I grew a bit more… and I transitioned into chaser. Ugh…

Now let me say that in the middle of a central Indiana summer there is no better place for a loose cow to hide and feed than in a field full of standing corn.

My father was a determined man who was always in charge of his realm. He was hard, and could be harsh when he got stressed or anxious. He had a way of shouting us into cooperation and obedience. It was not a "Yes, sir" world, but it was an environment that was difficult to feel like you had much choice.

By the time I was twelve I had come to really hate our farm fences. The perimeter areas were in bad repair and it was practically a sport for the animals to escape and go somewhere that required chasing.

This is the environment—the place and space—where my subconscious dropped me.

There I stood on the farm, being driven to the high standing cornfield where our cows were loose… again. My dad stood at the top of the hill overlooking the cornfield where he could see the rustle as animals moved through and destroyed his crops. He sent me and my sister into the field and shouted orders from his position to give us guidance. The corn stalks were razor sharp. The only way to get safely through the field was to go down one row with your arms crossed over your face. Of course to find roving animals, we had to cut *through* the rows, not just up and down them.

It was a miserable day and only getting worse. We were deep enough that Dad could do precious little but yell.

From the hypnotic comfort of my trance, I was not only remembering this event, but I was back in that cornfield all over again: the heat and the razor sharp assaults of the crops. Let me not fail to mention the fact that 900-pound animals are scary. What was I supposed to do if I actually found one? Where should I herd it? And *how?*

Add to that, Dad was agitated and yelling because we were not winning the battle.

It was at that point when I just stopped.

I remember thinking, "I'm done. I'm not running anymore. I hate corn, I hate cows, and I hate *running*!"

I was scared, I was tired, and for the most part I was totally done in. And in that moment I realized that I was in the middle of a cornfield. My Dad could not see me. He would never know whether I ran or not. In that moment the decision to run was mine. And I said, "NO."

That was the moment I decided to quit running and did not plan to run *ever again.* I had been standing in the middle of a cornfield, alone. I knew that I could not stay there but yet I had nowhere to go either.

That was the moment we had regressed to find.

Larry spoke with my subconscious. They carefully created a sequence of suggestions to take care of that dear child in the cornfield.

That was when the hypnosis magic began. Larry asked "me" to go into that field, with the knowledge I now have, and join that young girl. I did. I went and stood beside her and introduced myself. I told her that I was Sondra-of-the-future, that this day would end, and when she got older she would leave this farm and it would no longer be her day-to-day life.

I told her she would grow up to be a very intelligent, self-assured woman and it was all going to be okay.

Child-Sondra had surrendered that day to a situation which had been repeated so many times that she just quit. I took her by the hand—and as I did I felt her anguish, her pain, and her sense of being lost. I encouraged her that her father really did love her, but was just determined when a job needed to be done on the family farm.

I told her I would always be with her and to know in her heart that all this was temporary.

And she cried.

She cried the tears of a child being given a reprieve, knowing that something different was not only possible but *promised*.

Then Larry led me to hug this precious part of myself—who was in essence a memory buried deep within me—and ask her if she would like to come and live peacefully in my heart. That moment was a memory. It was okay for her to step away from the corn, to step away from the cows, to step away from the farm… and to come live with me in my heart.

She tearfully nodded yes.

With Larry's help, I held her in my arms. As I held on, she began to get smaller, and smaller, and smaller. She continued to shrink until she could stand on the palm of my hand. I cradled her there and walked us out of the cornfield, and into the life I now live, hundreds of miles away and decades later from that tough day.

Once we had her out of the field, Larry gave me the simple suggestion to place her into my heart so she would never feel alone again. We told her that running was not a requirement for her freedom, that she was just free and loved and safe and oh so precious.

When I think of that day now, I can still see it but there is no longer any emotion locked in the field. Did the cows ever make it back to the approved pasture? I don't remember. And I don't care. That was not the purpose of my journey.

On that day I had decided I was done running. I hated my life back then, but after this session that child-Sondra was free and on the road to profound healing.

I would like to tell you that after I healed from the traumatic moment that led me to stop running I suddenly decided to add jogging to my weight loss exercise routine.

But I didn't.

I still don't run, but not because I can't or I won't. I don't run because I *choose* not to. I prefer other forms of exercise.

A piece of my childhood was rescued that day, and for me, a broken piece of myself was brought home. Home to my heart, and all is well.

The Vault

(I Might Need a Bigger Box)

Larry and I had been doing lots of hypnosis practice. The choices and possibilities of things we could explore and discover continued to grow by the day.

We purposely did not chase every rabbit (or every cow!) that showed up, but some of them deserved to be revisited at a later date. Rather than make a spreadsheet of potential session points, another solution presented itself creatively.

While traveling to visit friends, we stayed at a nearby motel. As we were laying there with a few extra minutes we decided to have some hypno fun. I do not honestly recall where the experience began, but after a few minutes I rolled over and asked him to help me find a place to keep all of the things I still wanted to work on, or play with, later until we had time to get to them.

Since we had already created an "apartment" for visiting my subconscious, Larry suggested that Subconscious show me a place where we could store anything that had not yet been resolved.

She smiled and pointed to a door off the porch. *Who knew I had a porch?*

That is one of the magical elements of working with the mind. When a new component is needed, or even desired… voilà! There it is.

We went to the door and realized it held a vault. It was a space that only I had the code to open, a locked place for resolved and unresolved issues. As I looked inside, it had empty shelves on each wall. The door was like a Stargate, made of translucent material I could reach through without opening.

We spent a few minutes recalling hypnotic sessions where we bumped into items which still needed time and attention.

Bit by bit, I placed issues in boxes and shelved them on the yet-to-be-worked-through side. On the other, I placed stuff I'd already dealt with, but hadn't yet adjusted to being part of my new normal.

At one point I pushed my hands firmly into Larry's. He asked me what was happening. I told him there was a box. A box I wasn't ready to deal with yet. It was marked with a specific name and I was trying to shove the lid on it.

"I'm not sure, Larry, but I might need a bigger box!"

He laughed and asked Subconscious to help me get the lid on tight and tape it shut. *Mission accomplished.* We knew that on the day we would eventually open that box we were going to need a significant block of time.

After we finished our trance time and while I was getting ready for our upcoming visit, I put my face through that Stargate vault door… and just for fun tossed an apple core through.

Today, when I look inside, that apple core is still lying on the floor of my vault.

I don't actually use this tool much anymore. When we first started doing hypnosis I hadn't realized that challenges and issues can present themselves again if necessary. I didn't need to keep a list or spreadsheet—or even a vault—to keep track of them. I have since learned that our minds can and will bring forward anything that needs to be dealt with.

I have also learned that there is a system for creating a "new normal." As my mind settles into a position of healing, balance, or fresh alignment, the issues and challenges that brought about positive change are truly set free. With adjustments made at a deep level through a partnership between conscious and subconscious, the old is gone and the new has come through natural shifts.

Over and over and over again.

The only box still sitting in my vault is one I am very familiar with. The lid is on tight and covered with duct tape. Yes, perhaps one day I will deal with whatever remains in the box. But I hope by the time I have the guts to open it, most of the "stuff" will have already been dealt with, with only forgiveness waiting inside.

Pain Management

It Could Have Been Anything

I have shared with you the tools I chose to use for weight loss. In a few moments you will meet me along a different road as we traverse hypnotic pain management. Since this is my story you are going to learn through what I have encountered.

But it could have been anything.

Life is filled with issues and challenges that catapult us through monumental change. It could've been a fear of heights, or an aversion to certain smells, a desire to quit smoking, or the trauma and backlash of abuse.

Being a hypnosis subject has given me powerful tools for my benefit. It's not the only way, but it's the way I whole-heartedly recommend.

I simply want to share with you the magnitude of potential available when you say, "Hello, Subconscious. Will you partner with me for my highest and best interests?"

In the next section I share my experiences with pain, fear, surgeries, and recoveries. You will learn quickly how the mind (when paired with your subconscious) is so much better off together than alone.

You have already walked with me through profound life moments that have allowed me to look at pivot points as an invitation to live fully. The best is yet to come. Stick with me.

Acute vs. Chronic

One of the lessons we have learned while working with hypnosis is the phenomenal relationship our mind has with pain.

If pain is a result of hard-won achievement, we view it as a mark of success.

But when there's a meeting we don't want to attend, pain is an excellent excuse with secondary benefits... "Oh man, I'm sorry I can't make it. My leg hurts."

Pain is also a fabulous tool for extra attention and/or sympathy.

There are times when pain shifts to pleasure and it "hurts so good"—yoga stretches, lifting successively heavier weights, crossing the finish line of a marathon.

Hypnosis teaches that we also have the opportunity to stop—or at least slow down—our present circumstance to evaluate the sensation of pain.

One of my mentors teaches that we should always strive to live in the present moment. His example of how to get into the present moment is to hit your toe with a hammer... because no other time, past or future, will continue to matter.

I don't recommend the hammer, but you get the point.

Within hypnosis, we have the amazing opportunity to work with the subconscious. Working through the multitudes of cause and effects of pain to bring about positive change on a regular basis.

For many, pain is a constant companion. There are two primary types: acute and chronic.

Acute pain is that message given to us by our mind and body saying something is seriously wrong. Take a break, catch your breath and then diagnose whether or not further action is required for your overall health and well-being. Do you require medical attention? Would continuing this activity cause damage? Is your mind and body screaming at you, "*Enough* already?" If you have been injured, generally pain is associated. Your subconscious is more than willing to be of assistance in any way that is in your best interest. That is why it is always a good idea to check with your body before taking a pain reliever, just in case Body is giving you a very specific message.

Chronic pain is much different. It can be sporadic or constant, and often remains long after injury, surgery, or illness. It weakens the body, mind, and spirit.

Hypnosis assists with both acute and chronic pain.

In an emergency or urgent event, often times hypno can be helpful to calm the responses and shift focus from the pain to something that is less stressful. That does not remove the need to make an intelligent informed decision, but possibly a few deep breaths can and will be a relief.

Hypnosis can also assist in such a moment to shift into a let's-see-what's-happening mode with a clear option of watching how things progress. This story is one of those times for me.

My husband and I knew there was really no moment that could not be touched or enhanced by hypnosis.

While shopping at our local K-Mart it began to rain. It was dark and cold outside. Larry offered to go get the car while I waited on the curb. He pulled the car up beside me. I opened the rear door and realized he was not parked right next to the curb. As I stretched to unload something into the backseat, the item caught on the edge of the cart and pulled it off the sidewalk. With swift momentum the cart smashed into my hand, trapping it between the car door and the heavy cart, which I couldn't move because its front wheels were lodged at the drop to the curb.

Larry hurried from the driver's side and lifted the cart back in place. We both looked at my hand. It had already started to swell and that white line of impact was prominent.

Did I mention it really hurt?

We decided to park and take a better look at my shopping cart injury.

Larry gently took my hand into his and dropped me into hypnotic trance. Tears were close. He then spoke with my body and acknowledged that he knew my hand hurt. He asked my body to know that we were giving the issue our full attention. He asked Subconscious to shut off all pain in my hand for one hour.

In sixty minutes' time, he asked her to please turn the sensors back on. He only wanted enough time so my initial response could calm, so we could make an informed decision. Immediately my hand quit hurting, and as expected my awe and wonder of the power of hypnosis flowed through me.

As we pulled out of the parking lot, I looked at my hand. The swelling was rising quickly. I lifted my hand and showed it to Larry. "Man, I'll bet that really hurts right now but I don't feel a thing."

The bruise was showing up strongly though. We were mindful of the one-hour point, which found us home with the car unloaded.

My sensory systems came back online just as requested. My hand was okay. It was still a bit swollen and tender, but I could tell I had not broken anything.

Had I required medical care I have every confidence that we would have known to get it checked. This was merely soft tissue damage, and all was well. A bit of ice and appreciation for the wonders of hypnosis seemed to be all that were required.

I knew it was okay to accept the suggestion for the sensation of pain to be placed on hold temporarily. What this event accomplished was yet another reason for me to believe in hypnosis as my personal mind magic.

So Much for Straight Teeth

We looked at our flexible savings plan dollars one fall, and realized we needed to use more of the set aside money so we did not lose it.

One idea was to look into braces for me. My teeth have never been straight, but because I one day hoped to lead presentations, teach classes, and share my hypnosis experiences in public, braces got put on the "maybe" list.

Within a few days, I had an appointment with an orthodontist. I went for initial x-rays and consultation. When the doctor walked in with my results we assumed the biggest shock was going to be the price tag.

That was *not* the case.

She smiled and said, "Mrs. Lambert, your x-rays show a problem that will need to be dealt with by another dental professional before we can accept you as a client."

She laid my scans out on the table. I looked at the x-rays, and thought, "Oh dear God, please not again." I recognized what she was concerned about. There, within my left jaw bone, was a tumor.

I recognized it as a keratocyst—a rare and benign, but locally aggressive cyst which would have to be excised.

I knew immediately I would be headed back into excruciating jaw surgery for the third time in 20 years. Ugh.

To chase away the panic, we celebrated that the idea of braces had given us advance awareness that a cyst had reformed in my jaw.

Straight teeth were no longer the focal point.

I knew from past experience that this was a medical insurance issue, and as such, would not be handled by a dental surgeon. After several inquiries, I ended up at a surgeon's office with my x-rays in hand and had a pretty good idea of what was coming next.

I was uncomfortable and upset because the other two times I'd had a similar tumor removed, it had been incredibly painful. And the recovery sucked!

The doctor walked in, took one look at my films, and told me this surgery was way above her pay grade. I would need to find a super-surgeon.

She went on to say I did not have enough bone left to remove another tumor, and that this time I would lose half my face in the process. My jaw would have to be totally removed. They would probably be able to rebuild my face from my hip and leg. "Have a nice day."

She walked casually out of the room after ripping my life apart. And my face.

We sat there stunned and unsure what the proper response should be. Ultimately we chose for Larry to take me to the car for an emergency "Calm down" hypno session. Then he went back in to get referrals for another doctor who might be able to take care of our needs.

It was tough enough knowing the tumor was back, but knowing what the future would hold was devastating.

We drove home and started doing research on the surgery she had told us to expect. There was just no shallow end to the pool. We not only needed to locate an insurance-approved surgeon, but one who had the skill set I needed.

Larry and I also started pouring through the internet, hypnosis chat boards and social media sites to find advice on what type of hypnosis might be possible for such a procedure.

Pre- and post-surgical hypnosis is an established area of expertise within the realms of professional hypnosis, so we received lots of insight and learned how to prepare.

In preparation for a liquid diet, imposed by having my jaw wired shut, I purchased a Cuisinart juicer which stood on the kitchen counter as a reminder of an undesirable future.

The most beneficial hypnotic technique suggested was a process called Ultra Depth® which is a technique of James Ramey. The premise is that through the magic of hypnosis our minds are escorted to the core center where our bodies go to naturally heal. When we tap into healing at that level we experience our best and strongest chance for significant success.

As you might expect our next step was to find a certified Ultra Depth hypnotist to help me mentally cope with the medical ordeal to come.

The Tuesday night of our appointment, Laura West explained the concept to us. She would not only stage me to the deep end of healing within my mind and body, but would also work with Larry to be able to take me in and out of this state for the surgery itself.

It was the coolest thing. I entered into levels of profound relaxation, and then dropped to a level we simply called "healing."

With each new level she gave me a key word, that with intention, would take me instantly to that level of trance, complete with all its attributes.

One level allowed my body to not feel pain, another made suggestions for healing to become instantaneous.

Then she gave me a word, "Sunshine," to bring me back to the here and now, back to being fully awake and alert. The initial trance time took only a few minutes but she kept repeating it that day until it was clear that I had accepted the suggestions of trance depth perfectly.

Next she had Larry practice it a few times. The final stage was for me to simply think the key words with the intention of going "there."

It worked. I felt better equipped to deal with the idea of losing my face to tumor removal.

I now had hope that when the time came for the procedure, I would have exactly what I needed.

On Thursday morning I got up and ran my hands over my cheeks. I was astounded that the swelling had gone down significantly. I woke Larry up, excited because I had not even considered that after 90 minutes of Ultra Depth practice, my mind, body, and being had already begun the healing process.

Whatever my body had the ability to accomplish had been activated. Healing was flowing freely within me. I was shocked and amazed. I did a little happy dance right there in the bathroom, once again saying how much I love hypnosis!

Within a few days we were cleared to meet with a super-surgeon, Dr. Robert A. Ord, D.D.S., M.D., F.R.C.S., F.A.C.S. (All those letters after his name meant to us that he was skilled and equipped to do the facial reconstruction required for my situation.)

I was so nervous. I was carrying all the high level x-rays and reports. In walked an absolutely delightful man with a British accent who does this sort of thing all the time. He took a few moments to familiarize himself with my case, then casually set it aside and said, "You know, 85% of the people who sit in that chair lose at least a portion of their face. You, my dear, are not one of them. You are among the 15% who I can and for whom I will do something different."

I sat there and stared at him. Everyone we had spoken with, all the way up the chain to get into his office, had given us the same prognosis.

Caringly, he looked Larry in the eye and said, "You know, young man, if she were my wife this is exactly what I would do for her."

He explained that not only would I not have to have facial reconstruction, I would not even need surgery for quite a few months.

Again I sat there, stunned… and so relieved. There were no words.

He gave us a mini-class on the nature and behavior of a keratocyst. Yes, my jaw was thin. It could break very easily. "So don't pop yourself in the jaw," he said.

I agreed.

We were given an appointment time to return to his office, when he would insert a drain into the center of the cyst. I would spend the next six to nine months flushing it out with salt water, and he would monitor the cyst as it started to shrivel, shrink, and pull away from the bone in my jaw. Then after a number of months I would have a simpler surgery to go in and remove the seed of the tumor with no radical procedures required.

I don't know exactly how much healing the Ultra Depth suggestions created for me, but at that point I did not care. I was so happy. I was not going to lose my face!

I went home and looked at the new Cuisinart juicer on the counter, relieved that I would make juice because I *wanted* to, not because my jaw would be wired shut for months.

I went to work the next day elated that the guy trained to take my desk job while I recovered could stand down.

Larry and I then prepared for the hypnosis I would be using during the dental procedure which would ultimately be performed. We already had deep healing on our list, so we added a few other tools and techniques. Regardless of what we chose to do hypnotically, we would also respect the job everyone else had to do, and blend our modality to accommodate their procedure.

We arrived for the procedure on our appointed day. This time I was not scared. I was confident. All that was necessary would work out for my best.

The dental surgeon came into the room and explained what he and his assistant would be doing.

Larry asked his permission to explain what we would be adding to my experience. The doctor listened intently as my husband explained he would place me in a state of surgical hypnosis, and that I would be able to hear what was happening around me. I would only respond, however, if he spoke to me directly using my name.

We told him I had prepped well through hypnosis and what we were doing would be added on top of the surgeon and his assistant doing everything they would normally do during the procedure.

The surgeon was okay with that, and gave me the novocaine shot. He told Larry to begin whatever it was he was going to do.

Larry easily dropped me into a healing trance, gave me a kiss, and told me he would be right outside. He reminded the doctor that if he needed my attention he should call me by name and place his hand on my shoulder.

The procedure, although very important, went quickly. The surgeon talked through the whole thing, calling me "sweetie," or "honey," but avoiding my name.

We have laughed about that ever since. We assume he was scared to use my name or I might pop out of trance.

The surgeon told me about the drill, about the drain, about the stitches. Just that quick he touched my shoulder and said, "Sondra, we are finished," and I opened my eyes.

When Larry walked in the surgeon commented that if this is what was possible using hypnosis he wished they could hire Larry to assist with all their patients.

He discussed my post-op care and gave me an info sheet in case anything went wrong in the next few days. I was an active member of the conversation as we discussed the procedure and especially the hypnosis.

He wanted to know about my experience, which I was more than happy to share. We finished our conversation, with none of us realizing how talkative I had been. As he turned to walk out the door, I said to him in slurred words, "Doctor, my jaw is numb now. It's ready for you to begin."

He just shook his head and left the room smiling.

Ultra Depth rocks. It is a level of awareness that healing can happen all the time. When you take the time to place yourself in the space where healing happens, the process goes into overdrive.

To me that is its own form of magic.

This entire scenario began when I thought, "Hey wouldn't it be nice to have pretty, straight teeth?" We never did get back to the braces idea… mostly because (as it always seems to be), this was not the end of the story.

Dental Emergency

Rachel had come to spend the day with us, and I was not feeling well. We shared with her the incredible story of what happened at the dental surgeon's office approximately three days before.

It had been such a rush of hypnosis success and the stories were still fresh in our minds. She listened and we had a lovely visit. But as the day continued I just did not feel well. Kinda achy, kinda flu-ish and quite tired. I was not sick, I just did not feel my best.

Larry and I went to bed, and before too long the "ugh" returned. Sometime after midnight I awoke sick and shaky, and it seemed to be getting worse. I woke Larry and he began doing relaxation and calming hypnosis… whatever he could think of.

But still it continued to just get worse. I felt awful, then I got tremendously cold and started to quiver uncontrollably. I could hear Larry trying to soothe me with hypnosis. I was trying to be receptive but it was not working.

It became apparent that I was in need of medical assistance. I could not stop shaking, I felt like crap and my balance was off. We had a decision to make: call an ambulance, go to the nearest hospital, or throw me in the car and get back to University Hospital in Baltimore where they had done the dental procedure.

My condition was worsening by the moment, and fear set in. I was shaking so hard I couldn't speak clearly. I went into shock.

Larry called the "what if something goes wrong after your procedure" line and we were instructed to head to their facility as soon as possible.

He got me dressed, wrapped me in a blanket and got me into the car. The entire time he had not ceased using hypnotic suggestion and talking directly with my subconscious and my body. They gave him helpful insights as he multi-tasked to get us ready.

Then the most amazing thing happened.

He helped me into the vehicle, put the car in reverse... and I quit shaking. I calmed down and suddenly felt immensely better. Subconscious and Body knew I required medical attention, and they did not let the symptoms subside until we had made the decision to go to the hospital and were on our way.

During the thirty-minute drive to Baltimore, Larry steadily worked his hypnosis skills to the max and I felt profoundly better than I had in the house. The shaking was gone. It was no longer required to get our attention and coax us to make the right decision.

My mind and body worked in tandem to get me exactly where I needed to be.

In lightning speed we arrived at the emergency room. The doctors needed an accurate gauge of my pain and what was happening with my jaw. Since hypnotic suggestion was alleviating some of my symptoms, Larry needed to turn everything back on so they could make a diagnosis based on complete information... including the pain.

For the next few hours I was miserable. The pain was so severe they gave me IV medication every two hours. The facility is a teaching hospital, and in the middle of a weekend night I had every intern and student on emergency rotation, as well as the macio-facial rotation, coming in to poke and prod me.

I screamed, I cried, and I held onto Larry with everything I had. I floated in and out of consciousness as he sat beside me, now steadily working his hypno magic. As I looked into his eyes I knew I could slip in and out of consciousness, and he would be sane and strong, working on my behalf.

My husband used Ultra Depth to take me to a healing state. He kept tossing me into timelessness… so I could float beyond the pain as much as possible. He was also in continuous contact with my Subconscious and Body so the three of them could work through the ordeal to keep me as balanced and calm as possible.

We had been there for approximately eight hours. It was now morning, and my daughter Rachel came running into the room. She was like a ray of sunshine. I was calmed just to have her there.

She glared at her father and said, "Dad, there's a big difference between Mom being in 'Shock Trauma' and just the 'Emergency Room'." She was relieved but still shaken.

After she finished chastising her dad, she looked at me. I was so sick and in such pain. "Hi, Mama," she said. "What can I do for you?"

She rubbed my hair and held my hand. She also remembered all the hilarious details of my behavior to regale me later. One guy had poked my jaw and I grabbed his leg with a fist that brought tears to his eyes when I did not let go.

Ultimately it was determined that the plug which had been placed into the tumor was too big. Instead of draining it became a clogged infection-filled mess that needed to be removed.

The next morning my surgeon repaired the situation. I stayed in the hospital a couple of days on IV antibiotics and pain meds. I slept a lot. As bad as those few hours were, I do not want to imagine what I could have experienced without the powerful suggestions and hypnotic tools Larry used to keep me calm and relaxed.

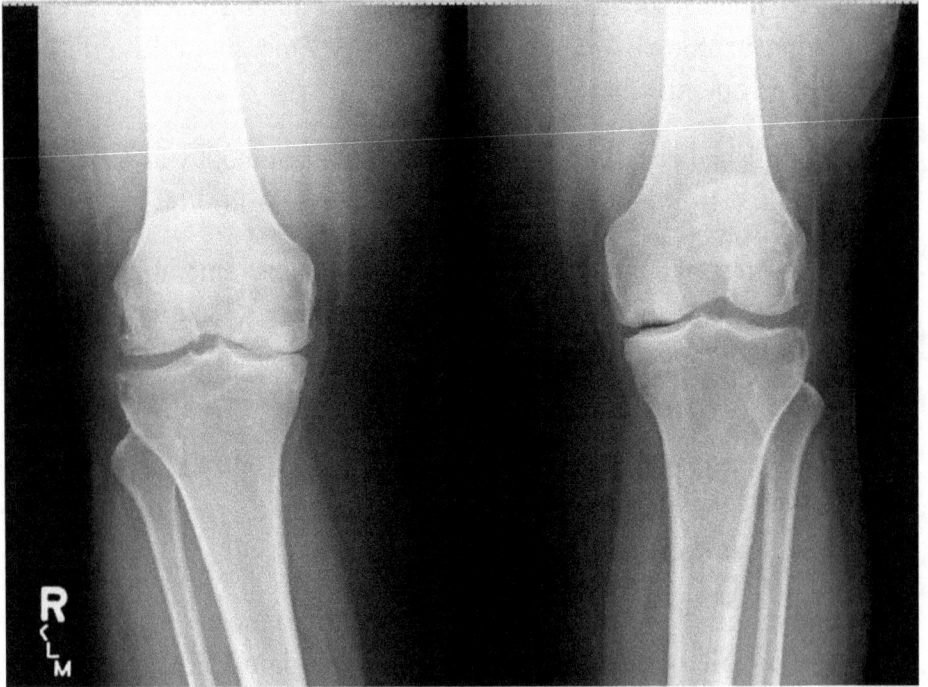

Ouch, My Knee!

I had knee surgery. I assumed there was no way recovery and rehab could possibly be as bad as how my knee felt before the procedure.

I was prepared hypnotically. We arrived at the surgical center. I was escorted into the prep area for the lovely gown and IV hook up. I was their second patient of the day and they were running on time, or even a little ahead of schedule.

When the doctor arrived to talk with us, he explained it was a simple procedure… one which he performed countless times each week.

My torn meniscus, with arthritis under the knee cap, was a piece of cake to him.

I was ready to get that phase of my life over with. *Just get it done*, I thought. *I have a life to live that does not include this.*

My husband and I spoke with the anesthetist. He was totally cool with Larry putting me into surgical trance, which is basically, "Subconscious, while Sondra is unconscious, you will give no attention to the sights, sounds, or experience of the surgery. I need you to follow the sound of my voice and 'Sleep now'."

Larry explained to the doctor that I could hear him and I would follow his instructions perfectly as long as they were directed at me intentionally and personally. All other spoken words in the room would neither be heard nor reacted to.

I heard the attendant ask me to slide from the bed I was in onto the surgical table, then he told me he was adding medicine to my IV. "We'll be taking very good care of you while you sleep."

I have had surgery several times before. When the go-to-sleep drugs hit my mind, it is always a bit of a rush. Perhaps a cross between an *ahhh* and a *wheee!*

It was over as fast as it began. What felt like a split second later, someone else was telling me it was finished.

Of course everything went well. All I needed to do was wake up a bit more, so my daughter and our friend Tammy could take me home. Larry had an important business meeting that day which could not be rescheduled. But I had plenty of love and support from my girls.

I sat up. The nurse asked me what my pain number was—between 1 and 10. She offered me Demoral for the ride home.

I started to tremble. The shaking was rough and I got scared. Without skipping a beat, Rachel got her dad on the phone and asked him what my trigger word was to "Calm me down."

Rachel is not a hypnotist. She's not even certain that it's something she's fully comfortable with. But when it comes to her mama, she knew what I believed. She knew for me, there was power and truth in hypnosis.

I heard Rachel's voice in my ear as she triggered me saying, "Dad says to say…"

I immediately quit shaking and I was not cold anymore.

Rachel looked at me like I had two heads. I also saw a flicker of "Man, this shit works" in her expression.

The girls got me home, properly drugged, with my knee elevated above my heart.

Larry had already prepped me with ample hypnosis for my initial recovery hours. I would "drift, float, dream, and allow the meds to take their full effect while I enjoyed an afternoon of going into the playground of my mind, allowing Subconscious to handle everything else." *Game on!*

I felt no need to actually sleep because the pain meds did not include sedatives. It was more of an afternoon high.

I had cooked, cleaned, and prepared everything ahead of time for a smooth couple of days. My friend Tammy watched over me.

At one point she said she was going to get up.

Later she told me I laughingly said, "No, stay here. Dance in the rainbows with me!" She said I went into a long and detailed scenario about going to our special lake and watching the orange origami fish swim and jump and play. As the fish swam the water became filled with healing magic.

Tammy decided it might be in our best interests if she stayed put while I was "high as a kite."

Upon those words, of course, I started flying kites in my head—big ornate ones with long tails—in a beautiful blue sky. One of them may have even been shaped like a bright orange origami fish!

Those first few days were cumbersome but not too difficult. As expected, the post-surgery pain was not as bad as it had been before surgery.

The pain meds and regular hypnosis worked in tandem. The specific hypnotic suggestions changed over time, as new pain and healing needs made themselves known. A few days after surgery, when the tight wrap had been removed, my thigh was absolutely screaming. Larry ran pain trances through me like water. Although I was listening and following his simple instructions, my leg still hurt. Simple suggestion could only go so far without knowledge of exactly what we were working on. Blessed pain meds!

Our research discovered the thigh pain I was experiencing was because blood flow through my knee had been cut off during the procedure, and restricted by the tight wrap. Now a few days later my thigh felt the deep painful bruising from the tourniquet.

With this knowledge we had a direction to take the healing hypnosis. We spoke to the needs of the muscles, the veins, and did a bit more research.

That evening my body was so relieved. We wrapped my thigh in warm towels soaked in mineral salts. Hypnosis is a HUGE and amazing tool, but it is not intended to be a stand alone solution for everything.

I assumed recovery would go smoothly and my knee would be so appreciative of the focused attention. The orthopedic surgeon had told me more than once that because there was arthritis in my knee, that would impede my recovery.

Physical therapy began after about a week. Larry went with me for the initial assessment, so we would better understand what kind of hypnosis might be appropriate for the situation. The surgeon had also suggested I take the super-duper pain drugs before therapy sessions for the first week or so. I was not going to need that!

The doctor had specifically asked for aggressive range of motion and quad strengthening. The therapist started her assessment and began the first of several sessions where I literally screamed and cried out because it hurt so bad.

When she finished bending my knee the first time, Larry stepped in and asked for a moment. He dropped me into healing trance and then asked her to try again.

My knee bent much easier and farther. She was amazed at the difference.

"Can she still feel pain? Because that's important at this stage."

He explained that I would feel anything that could or would actually injure me. Any other pain was placed into a subdued healing mode.

She didn't seem entirely comfortable with his explanation but she also didn't argue with the truth of what she had just witnessed.

I returned for physical therapy three times a week, and for the first couple of weeks I pulled away from her every time she did the range of motion stretches. I went home whining how much it still hurt and that what we were doing was not going to stop the deep bruises and veins from needing time to heal.

Hypnosis does not, will not, and should not numb nor diminish pain that is centered for your highest and best good. If there is an issue that requires medical attention, your body will win that argument every time.

We all have our own relationship with pain. Pain like everything else in our lives is unique and it is ours. No one can take it from us. At the same time we have the invitation to co-create a partnership with pain that allows life to happen to the very best possible result.

Hypnosis continues to help me help myself, by shifting my perspective into a place and space of balanced alignment. Sometimes that is all pain requires. However, when pain requires a mind with body agreement, plus medical assistance, pay attention. The quality of your life may depend upon it.

Defining Mission Critical

Change can be as simple as realizing there are many ways to get through the challenges. A clear view of what is possible is always nice. Making informed choices clear is what makes momentum flow forward. It is in the navigation and the creation of the momentum that your hypnotist becomes mission critical.

From time to time someone will come to me and ask me to "fix" them. They have tried "everything they could think of" and nothing has worked.

I am always excited because change is just a few moments of fresh perspective away.

It is important to note that hypnotic change occurs when your subconscious is invited to join in co-creating possible solutions. A good hypnotist is essential to assist and guide the process of positive change or healing. As long as that connection is clear and strong between you and your hypnotist, the spoken and unspoken, the seen and the unseen will reveal themselves throughout the course of the sessions.

The role of your hypnotist is to lead you into a state of relaxation with the intention of collecting data, exploring what is being presented to you, and then helping you recognize what has been discovered.

You as the subject are the one who makes the changes. The hypnotist facilitates, escorts, and assists.

It is magical to be allowed to witness the changes when they occur. Releasing fear, accepting fresh perspectives, allowing healing to happen, and setting up the necessary tools to return for more information in the future.

A great hypnotist develops a connection with clients which is similar to joining them on their journey as their guide and escort… especially when the best course of action is forgiveness.

It is infinitely easier to "listen to the sound of my voice and follow simple instructions" than it would be to confront an issue or someone who has wronged you in the past by yourself. In areas of self-image, self-worth, and self-sabotage, it is important to have a steady voice to listen to as you flow through the guided options.

Healing is multifaceted with more layers than can be counted, and since we have hypnosis, counting those layers is not necessary. The partnership that flows for healing, is as simple as listening to the sound of my voice and following my simple instructions.

If you bump into something painful or unexpected you can always be brought back out. After a strategy session you can then go back in informed. There is no rush, nor expectations placed upon your healing. it is exactly that… *yours*.

You can go into the healing pool, or to a garden that needs to be weeded, or you can pack boxes, close them with duct tape, and send them off to be incinerated. Healing and wholeness are partnered at the heart. Neither is far from the other.

What good would it do you if someone else "fixed" you?

The magic is in receiving the gifts given from within yourself and then walking on into the newness of your life.

You have read my stories, and you know that until I partnered with my subconscious to face the tough stuff, I would not have been able to build the bridges necessary to get across the raging rivers alone.

My hypnotist may have been mission critical… but not because that person fixed me… rather because they made change possible.

Make It So

Livin' the Dream

I frequently tell people the best gift my husband ever gave me was the day he became my personal hypnotist. It was an opportunity to live the life of my dreams.

I dream, we interact, and the result is living with fresh perspective. What wife would not like that?

Through the experiences which introduced me to hypnosis, my husband and I began to see my life transform.

The traumatic nightmare of 15 years was released, I had reduced my weight by 70 pounds, discovered a sensual side to Sondra, and met and found a best friend in my subconscious.

It was obvious I had found a passion for my inner mind. Countless positive changes began happening at the speed of thought. I actively looked for other things that I could use hypnosis to improve.

Larry (who loves me from his heart) made a decision. He decided that it would be more cost effective to become a certified hypnotist than continue to pay others to hypnotize me. It was not a judgment of other hypnotists, it was a fiscal issue filled with his love for me.

We called a hypnotist friend and asked for his advice on a training school. He said there were several excellent certification programs. His own mentor had been a graduate of the Omni Hypnosis Training Center in Deland, Florida, created by master hypnotist Jerry Kein. After much research we chose to follow this advice and got Larry scheduled for the next certification class.

Before you judge, I will tell you that until this point in my journey, Larry was as far from "Woo Woo" (his term) as anyone you've ever met. He is a 20-year veteran of the US Army and had been a defense contractor for nearly 15 years.

But we had personally experienced a transformation through hypnosis, and his interest was piqued enough to learn from the best of the best.

Larry is also one of those men who never does anything halfway. If it is worth doing, it is worth doing well.

Now years later he owns, operates, and is the lead instructor for the Omni Hypnosis Training Center of Washington, D.C. It is his greatest passion to share with others what we have added into our own lives.

Don't Be Controlled by Tears You Will Not Cry

There are pivot points in our everyday lives. Most we ignore or choose to blend into our normal activities. Others we take an extra moment to give special attention and realize we've been given an opportunity for positive change.

I had been an avid hypnosis subject for quite a while. My husband Larry had become a certified hypnotist—and my own personal service provider—and he even had a few clients in a home-based business while we continued to live our day-to-day lives.

Of those personal clients, for me, Beth was the most profound. She was referred to Larry for an in-person session by another hypnotist who lived too far away. She was heartbroken after her husband had passed away three months earlier, yet she had not yet been able to cry.

Because privacy is 100% imperative, Larry worked with her alone, but after quite a while, he opened the door and asked me to join them. He explained Beth was still struggling. He thought possibly I could add an element to the session she needed.

I asked Beth if I could sit beside her as she shared her challenge. She said she wanted our help and whatever I could add was appreciated.

Larry escorted her back into trance. I looked her in the eye, told her I would be with her through it all and held her hand. It took a few moments to realize that a shift was happening within her. She began to let go of the wall she perceived as holding her tears back. It came down gently. The emotions of a broken heart started to release the pent up tension and pressure.

Then came the tears she so sincerely had asked us to help her find.

She finally cried the tears of a grieving widow with intense emotion. I held her in my arms as Larry's hypnotic trance work began to set her free from her personal prison. She cried from the depths of her being and said goodbye to her beloved—all while feeling safe and secure.

Beth began to heal her broken heart. She would finally be capable of getting on with her life. She would later say it was my presence that ultimately brought the wall down, and allowed her to release once we established a safe zone.

That day Beth chose not to be controlled by the tears she could not—or would not—cry.

That required a moment of courage combined with a willingness to allow healing to happen. I was able to ask questions from a woman to woman point of view. She grasped onto that newfound comfort level which allowed her to open a door previously closed tight. She listened to the sound of my voice and from deep within her, Beth's subconscious found a voice of her own she could use to turn the key and unlock the tears.

That was the moment I knew I no longer wanted only to be a hypnosis subject. My life was intended to create a relationship with hypnosis beyond just being in trance. I wanted to be a certified hypnotist as well, and I wanted to see "CHt"—Certified Hypnotherapist—on business cards behind my own name.

Beth and I have discussed that evening many times since. She is now a good friend, and was able to remarry two years later.

I have also worked with both of her kids. With her young son we found four great things he could do when he gets angry. At the end of his session, he got his crayons and drew us a picture of what he had learned.

It went on his frig immediately. He was able to use his "get mad" steps successfully in the months which followed.

Her daughter and I used her love of reading to create better sleeping habits. We discovered that the placement of her stuffed animals could be key for her. She does not see her imagination, she feels the things she imagines. We gave the animals their assignments knowing that she would feel their loving care as she slept soundly through the night. Also the really big stuffed buddy had to sleep at the end of the bed so she had enough room to wiggle. Great kids indeed.

Beth, like me, gravitated to the powerful possibilities available through hypnosis. She created a life for herself that included deep healing and life-transforming change. Beth is now remarried to a man who loves her and has also become a hypnotist. There is a certain amount of, "Man, if this is what is possible, I want it too."

Her new husband became a hypnotist while they were dating as a gift to her from his heart.

National Guild of Hypnotists

Merrimack, New Hampshire

This is to certify that _Sondra Lambert_ having satisfactorily completed the required studies, has been found by the Board of Directors to possess the qualifications required by Constitutional by-laws, and is hereby registered as

Certified Hypnotist

In Witness Whereof, the Signature of the Administrator is

hereunto affixed on this ____ day ____ January ____ 20__

Certified Hypnotherapist

After meeting and sharing the session with Beth, it was an easy decision for me to transition from being only a hypno-subject into the role of facilitator and hypnotic guide. I was already married to and living with the best hypnotist on the planet (I am allowed to be biased) and I could learn with and through him. I also received my training through Omni Hypnosis Training Center and Jerry Kein.

The transformational shifts and changes had been substantial. It seemed there was always more profound potential ahead.

So Larry and I had some important decisions to make. It was abundantly clear that hypnosis had changed our lives for the better, and this was only the beginning.

A few months after I got my certification, a new training school opened—Hypnosis Practitioner Training Institute (HPTI). Its mission was to have the field's elite teach what they know and do best to a select group of students who would spend 500 hours dedicating themselves to this level of expert instruction.

The course instructor, Scott Sandland, is a nationally recognized expert in the fields of Medical Hypnosis, Pain Control, and Dental Hypnosis.

I remember my first day in California for the HPTI on-site training. We split into groups and were instructed to do a hypnotic induction using whatever word was given to us by the guy in line behind us.

I received the words "hot air balloon."

I was standing in front of a man named Dave who stared me down. His facial expression said it was a competition—I was not going to win.

It was at that moment that I first I understood hypnosis is a state of 100% consent.

That was a great first lesson to learn.

I asked Dave to close his eyes and imagine he was rising higher and higher in a hot air balloon. As the balloon rises, you relax deeper and deeper. When I brought the balloon back down and asked him to open his eyes, he looked at me and started to explain how I had done it all wrong.

The hypnotic induction gave him precisely the experience he expected it would. It had not worked at all.

His loss.

Galaxy Hypnosis

Larry and I raised our three kids as he served our country in the United States Army. We had the opportunity to have an extraordinary life.

The years following Army retirement introduced us to the world of government contractors. Larry took a position with the Department of Defense, while I became an expert on mass transportation at the Department of Transportation. The kids went to the colleges of their choice, the tuitions got paid, and all three got married.

I would not have traded even one moment.

I went to work at DOT to pay the kids' tuition. Our son became a project manager at the Pentagon, and our daughter an executive news producer with ABC. It took me twelve years of dedicated effort to pay off the student loans. My mission was successfully accomplished.

Larry and I had a drive and determination to create a hypnosis business for ourselves as our next adventure.

We were both now certified professionals. Our lives truly belonged to us. There was nothing we wanted more than to share with others what we ourselves had received and achieved.

When a meeting was called at DOT to announce my department would be reduced by six people, I spoke with my supervisor and asked to be placed on the layoff list. I was one of the only people who left feeling free in doing so. On my last day—after 12 years—I clocked out and drove home into a world of fresh possibilities as a small business owner.

Galaxy Hypnosis was born.

Renovations created a stunning office and location. Family and friends worked with us for a month. We hit the ground running and have not stopped since. Larry kept his contract position so we would still have some money coming in as we built our practice and client base.

We worked with several military members and their families to deal with issues that, in one way or another, were connected to Iraq and Afghanistan deployments. We were determined to make tools available to them which had freed us personally.

Around that same time Jerry Kein—with whom we had both trained at OHTC—announced his upcoming retirement. He would hold one last class through which he would train the trainers and franchise Omni Hypnosis Training Center to those whom he trained to go forth with his passion for excellence.

It took us less than one conversation to decide Larry should be in that training class. My husband had spent more than half of his Army career as an instructor, and he respected Jerry absolutely. This would also give our business the opportunity to help others become certified hypnotists. We could make a significant contribution to the growth of our profession.

It was a win.

Galaxy Hypnosis has became the home of Omni Hypnosis Training Center of Washington, D.C., located in Crofton, Maryland.

My husband is an amazing instructor. He looks you in the eye and teaches from the heart. He is able to instruct with authority, integrity, and a wealth of personal experience. His students have come to us from Indiana, Tennessee, Virginia, Pennsylvania, West Virginia, Maryland, the District of Columbia, and China. For those who are successful we offer an invitation to become a satellite office of Galaxy Hypnosis upon completion of their certification.

Many have said they see our biggest success as the combination of a husband and wife hypnosis team who work together successfully. (Apparently there are not a lot of those out there.)

Larry and I have very different styles. Larry is a strong direct suggestion hypnotist, with an uncanny rapport with his subjects. He is energetically connected with his clients in such a way, and does not shy away from the tough stuff people are ready to get rid of.

I, on the other hand, am much more likely to lead my clients down a path for health, healing, and wellness that I know works—because it has worked for me.

Larry goes by the book, I go with my personal experiences as a subject. Both are powerfully effective, just a different approach to the same goals.

Broken Pieces

I have mentioned in many of my stories that through the magic of hypnosis, another broken piece came home. This is the story of how that metaphor came into being.

In the role of hypnotist I have had the amazing privilege of meeting others in our profession, and I have probably been hypnotized by more of them than anyone else I know.

Some work best when using a pre-written script—with words that have been proven to be powerful and effective. Some scripts are copyrighted work which must be followed precisely to insure the expected outcome. This is a brilliant way for the genius of one hypnotist to be duplicated by others. When Laura staged me for Ultra Depth she read verbatim from the approved script and my results were nothing less than brilliant.

Many hypnotists have a strong preference to be in total control of the session. They use the "I talk, you do" approach. Their words are carefully chosen and the flow of the session is expected to meet expectations by its form and function. The "I talk, you do" also works great. Once rapport is established during the pre-talk there is a clear understanding that much of what will be accomplished will be based on direct suggestion. The words spoken, the inflection of the voice and the environment is carefully controlled.

Then there are hypnotists who build a personal rapport with their clients that does not require a script. They even encourage a partnership of communications. This is the camp I prefer to work within whether hypnotist or subject. When the guide can use the tools and techniques fluidly, and can shift directions in the blink of an eye, the subject is free to drift and float from one scenario to another from within.

Some hypnotists have spent a career developing their own personal style. Knowing that the effects are solid and repeatable brings about positive change for their subjects.

All hypnotists are passionate people who have the goal of being the guide, being the assistant, being an escort for others who seek change within themselves. We all know it is actually the client/subject who makes the changes. We give suggestions, we give tools, we suggest change work and the one we are helping makes the actual transformation.

I know several professionals from each of these hypnosis styles. For me—since I have such a personal partnership with my subconscious—I prefer to work with those who are willing to openly communicate with my subconscious as a partner. Those who are willing to ask her questions and listen to insights from her point of view and unique ability to bring the hidden to light in a balanced way with full awareness.

There are a few hypnosis social media sites and through them it is easy to meet others from around the country and even around the world. It was through one of these sites that I met a hypnotist from across the country. He is an interesting mix of the types and styles I mentioned earlier. He likes talking to my subconscious, but also clearly likes to lead the session with a "you do" attitude. We started to share hypno sessions via phone calls and it was always a thrill to spend an hour or so on a Saturday enjoying hypnosis together.

On one occasion he spent time figuring out how my mind works. We were not doing deep therapy. As if given the invitation my subconscious began to show him the twists, the turns, and the "map within me."

At one point he suggested I go deeper. I recognized that I was standing in a mine shaft, with several different paths and choices. All along the walls were shiny stones that seemed to glisten just right to show me the best path to explore. This was cool. I reached out to touch one of the stones and realized they were diamonds.

My mind had transformed itself into a maze in a diamond mine.

Without skipping a beat I began to sing, "Hi Ho, Hi Ho, it's off to work we go."

"Okay, what did you find and where are you now?" he asked.

After that session he began to use the image of a diamond when he worked with me… of course one which was mined from my own mind-mine. Perfect. It was personal and self-generated yet available to be revisited.

About a year later we had the opportunity to meet in person at a weekend seminar. Since we had done lots of work together already, there was no need to start from the beginning. We had been using what we came to refer to as "Diamond Energy," where we invited my subconscious to dig deep and bring forth anything that would be better after healing or change work.

We worked with weight loss, self-esteem, professional development, healing of memories, releasing old crap, and escorting in new perceptions.

He told me he wanted to try something fresh he had been working on. *Game on!* You know how I like to be a hypno guinea pig.

The suggested environment for this session was a magic bubble. Once inside this bubble there would be Diamond Energy everywhere and its magic would be phenomenal. It was a place of light and love, of acceptance, awareness, knowledge, and safety.

I slipped into that bubble with ease, and as I looked around there was beautiful, bright light everywhere. But unlike most bright lights this did not bother my eyes. From inside the bubble, the world outside looked opaque, like a child's soap bubble floating in the summer sun. I heard music with a vibrational beat that seemed to center upon me. It felt like I was being balanced and cleared all at the same time. It was warm and fun and casual. There were no rules or expectations, it was a place of peace.

I looked up and hanging from the center of my bubble's top was a silver disco mirror ball. As it spun the reflections were images of me dancing around, bouncing off surfaces.

Then the music stopped and I heard something like a herald trumpet, announcing the arrival of someone or something special. I turned and watched as two massive doors were opened.

One door was being opened by Perfection, the other by Compassion. The doors opened wide and a parade of what I would come to call my "broken pieces" walked, danced, and sauntered into the huge room. I knew immediately they were pieces of me that had been left behind, or were lost or stolen.

My shattered pieces were coming home.

As they entered they instinctively went into one of three places.

The first group came in and immediately knew who they were and where they fit. They absorbed into my present life—my memories, my hopes, and dreams—and were welcomed home with great joy. I did not have any definitions for what was taking place. I just watched them go home. I would later learn who and what many of them were. Yet all my broken pieces knew who they were, whether I recognized them or not.

The second group floated in and did not seem to have anywhere to go. They swirled together as I watched them form into a stunning mandala. It was beautiful, each individual joining a collective piece of exquisite art. That mandala glistened in the light of the reflective mirror ball.

The third group was the most fun. They gathered under the reflective ball and just partied. They identified themselves as those pieces of me who would have belonged with issues I had already resolved. They said that they were just there to party. And they danced the night away. They appreciated being brought home and they appreciated being among the chosen. Their job, however, was already done.

How cool is that?

I stood there in awe and wonder as all of me came home. No definitions were required, no expectations, no rules. It was a welcome home party of magnitude which I hosted effortlessly. It was as smooth and easy as breathing in, then breathing out.

I came out of trance and was fascinated. I asked my friend how his Bubble technique was working for him, since I was his first complete test subject. He smiled and said, "As far as I can tell, it was a phenomenal success."

What I came to learn in the following weeks, months and years was that the first and third groups were pretty self-explanatory. They either fit into the now or their mission had been accomplished. The ease of filling missing details into my current life made everything more clear and gave me a wider view and richer perspective for making decisions.

It was that second group that became the most fascinating, however. The mosaic of Sondra's broken pieces turned out to be the pieces—the issues—that arrived before I knew I needed to summon them. Even now, years later, there will be something that I am dealing with and something is just not quite right, not quite finished. I struggle to get a clear grip on a situation or circumstance, and POOF as if by magic one or more of the broken pieces from the mosaic will hop down and insert themselves. The remaining pieces swirl again and the mosaic of me is just a bit different, yet still just as authentic.

My broken pieces came home knowing that one day I would be ready for them to come into perfect placement in my life.

So as you read my writings and hear my stories, when I use the phrase "and another broken piece found her way home," it is this experience I am talking about.

As often happens among friends, that hypnotist and I went in separate directions and lost track of each other, but the powerful presence of the magical bubble remains with me as a constant companion. He gave me my bubble and within it lives all of me, the broken, the completed, and the work in progress.

And the doors are being guarded by Perfection and Compassion.

In the Blink of a Belief

I recently attended a class called "The Colors of Our Lives."

The speaker explained that at birth, we do not have any concept of color or its significance. As we grow and learn, we are taught to recognize color within our world. We accept the parameters of its definitions. He also pointed out that color groups are recognized differently throughout the cultures of our world.

He shared that there are some people in Africa who recognize a color specifically named for a particular green plant. It is rare and unique in their world. We would call it "green," yet when they see it the shade is as different as green and blue appear to us.

Not only is the concept of color learned, but afterword we come to believe it as absolute truth. What we believe to be the color red, must be red because... well... it's *red*.

I shared with the instructor that I had been looking through the multitude of Sherwin Williams palettes to select colors to paint my house. It didn't take long before the subtle shift of hues and shades challenged my simple definitions of colors seen as Red, Green, Blue, or Yellow.

I have chosen Storm Cloud, Krypton, Nugget, River Rock, Uncertain Gray, and Inviting Ivory. I am not color-challenged. I am free.

Welcome to the fascinating realm of belief systems.

Color is a simple example of something we believe as absolute. Once defined, it's a belief which smoothly and easily weaves its way into the rest of our life.

Many times when asked, "What do you believe?" the answer brings up areas surrounding faith.

We answer, "I believe in…"

It doesn't take much discussion to realize most of the things we consider ourselves to *believe* are not original thoughts. They are patterned behavior, adapted for a balanced life, or to fit into the expectations of others.

When the opportunity presents itself to examine what you believe (and more importantly *why*), it opens up a unique opportunity for you to create a fresh point of view. A view based on your choices and possibilities, where limitations are set free and allowed to shift or change.

I recommend we all examine what we believe, *why* we believe it, and whether or not it is something that still serves our lives to our fullest potential.

Some of the beliefs we needed as children no longer serve us well. They are ready to be either shifted, changed, or dismissed. Others will allow us to reach beyond our dreams, and launch into yet to be discovered possibilities.

Within hypnosis, limitations can quickly be redefined.

The "I can't" becomes "I don't believe I can," and leads us to question "What might be possible if I realized I'm no longer required to hold on to that belief which no longer fits into my highest and best interests?"

When you discover the origin of what you've "always" believed, you'll stand at the edge of a much freer future.

Is that limiting belief still necessary? *No, thank you. Goodbye!*

"When you look at something differently, what you look at changes"

The fantastic journey that began the first time I said "Yes" to hypnosis set off a chain of events that can only be described as incredible, positive momentum. Once the fuse was lit the path was illuminated.

I have woken up every morning for years with a willingness to ask questions, give my attention to the responses, then willingly take action on the choices and possibilities offered to me. It has been built with practice and dedicated focus—mixed with a willingness to laugh. Laughter invites the heaviness to dissipate safely.

The phrase "When I look at something differently, what I am looking at changes" has become a mantra for me.

Shifts of focus do not require major adjustments. A series of simple small ones works best. Imagine the fine tuning with a pair of binoculars to bring a distant image into focus. It's like the choice to look at the sunshine instead of the shadows while standing in the exact same spot, or the choice to listen to what is being said instead of just hearing the words being spoken.

I met my subconscious, and in doing so immediately began a relationship with my best friend. I don't feel empty or less than other people anymore. I meet each day with an attitude of gratitude, I breathe deeply both in and out, while knowing I am never alone.

I take me with me everywhere I go.

I did not have to travel far along this path to realize it was something worth sharing—something of sincere value that I wanted to give as much as receive.

So I started sharing with anyone who could hear me or would listen to what I had to say. My enthusiasm has been characterized as infectious. These personal stories resonate with others and my heart resounds with the passion I have for living life freely.

It is okay to look at your life and desire a new normal. It is okay to choose to create positive change then walk into it with confidence. It is okay to heal in a world that is hurting, and it is okay to take care of yourself as a priority. I have done it and I honestly say, "It works." It is worth the shifts in perspective that are required to get there.

When others were being laid off at my workplace, I requested the severance, handed in my ID badge, got in the car, and drove home to become a full-time hypnotist. I have not regretted the decision nor have I looked back.

Sometimes walking into a dream seems vague. That is where the good stuff is, that means that all things are possible and I can and will follow the positive momentum.

We often laugh at how different Larry and I are as hypnotists. He likes to face the issues, get to the root of the problem and knock it out of the park. I prefer to recognize the issues, say thank you for their faithful, loyal attention, and then invite them to leave.

Both approaches work brilliantly, just from different perspectives. I tell our clients: "Larry wrestles bears, I tame them."

Our clients wind up with a well-rounded approach that, in one or both ways, assists them on their personal journey into freedom.

For those who feel or think hypnosis is just a bunch of hocus pocus, I warn you that if that is your truth, then what you expect is what you will get.

For those willing to open their hearts and minds to believe it will work for them, there is nothing better. When you take the time to have a sincere relationship with the part of you who takes care of you 24/7, the partnership will allow you the same illuminated path I continued to enjoy.

You do not have to go through hell and back to find it. It is a path that will find you if only you let it.

Hypnotists—like everyone else in the world—come in various sizes, shapes, specialties, strengths, and weaknesses. Take the time to find a good one for you.

Client Stories

Exploring Expectations

One of the most significant moments we have the privilege of sharing with our clients is the initial conversation, generally called a pre-talk. This is when we get a chance to enjoy a shared interview process. We get to know them, they get to know us.

There are a list of things that are crucial for a successful session to follow.

There are several myths about hypnosis. We discuss the fact hypnosis is not sleep. To the outside observer, it appears the subject is a relaxed sleeping person. The hypnosis subject however, knows differently. You are *not* sleeping.

The second important difference between expectations and reality is that you can hear the sound of my voice.

What good would it do if you could not hear me? When I am speaking with your subconscious, she needs to be able to hear, process, and respond. The guidance I give my clients is this: "Listen to the sound of my voice and follow my simple instructions. When we agree that you will listen to me and I will keep it simple, then we can begin with a verbal contract that allows the session to flow smoothly."

I cannot count the number of times a client has emerged from a profound experience that created monumental opportunities for positive change only to say, "I don't think I was hypnotized because I heard every word you said and I remember it all."

You will hear my voice, the change occurs as you follow along while being relaxed. Sometimes I will have someone open their eyes while we are working together. Eyes open hypnosis is just as powerful—and sometimes more so—due to the fact we get around that pesky "I heard you" hurdle.

One of my clients is a nationally ranked ice dancer. Because she lives her life laser-focused, trance occurs most profoundly when her mind and attention are allowed to be directed on something with her eyes open. I encourage her to play games on her cell phone during our sessions. As her critical attention is drawn to the game strategy, her subconscious is free to finally relax into her own definition of trance. It works. Last year she made it to Nationals and has qualified this year as well.

Many do not grasp that while I am working with their subconscious, the conscious thinking mind is invited to drift, float, and dream, but is not ever excluded. She is welcome to participate. The magic of thought is not shut off when trance time begins. That's where the good stuff is.

When that connection is created well—and with multiple modes of communication in place—it is a win-win for all. Sometimes she will communicate at the speed of thought, other times by developing signals, allowing you to notice things in your world for the first time even though they have always been there. A message or a sign, perhaps something repeated throughout your day.

I realize that the entertainment business has created a scenario which is not helpful to hypnotherapists. If you expect it to be like a stage show, or how it's portrayed in the movies, then your first session will give you another opportunity to say, "Wow, that's not what I expected."

Will you remember everything which occurs in a session?

This is a very interesting question.

Hypnotists never work toward intentional amnesia. It would not serve anyone's best interests to ask or expect a person to block out information from the session.

With that said, it is also not required for you to remember all the details. It is best to let the information just flow. If you have total recall afterwards, cool. But if you have gaps, that's perfect as well.

Your subconscious does not miss anything, ever.

One of my favorite hypno related jokes is, "You remember 100% of what you remember."

As a subject, time distortion is so much fun. Trance time can seem as a moment or an hour has gone by, or you can sort through decades of life, solve the problems of the world and still be home for dinner. Time, place, and space are not relevant during hypnosis.

I always begin a session by asking what time the subject needs to leave my office. I promise to watch the clock. I keep my cell phone on the floor beside my chair and activate it with my toe during our session to time things as necessary. This allows the recipient freedom to accept the gift of time distortion, without the normal worries and concerns imposed by agendas and ticking clocks.

Another important thing to realize as a subject is that you never leave the real world. If you started in the chair you will be in the chair when you return. You can expect the sounds of life to continue. Your hypnotist will encourage you to relax into the knowledge that the sounds around you will only serve to relax you more. You will know you are safe, secure, and all is well. Traffic or office conversations just do not matter.

As I bring someone back to awareness in my office, I also prepare them to awaken refreshed, relaxed, and feeling totally amazing. I usually point out something about the sound of the air flowing through the vents again. That is an easy return-to-reality point.

This next myth is one of my favorites: It is not possible to get stuck in a hypnotic state.

Since communications happen directly through your subconscious mind, and her number one job is to function with your greatest interests at heart, there is nothing I could say or do to override her internal radar for you.

If I ever said or did anything that violated your trust she would pop you out of trance immediately. She is vigilant. That is why the partnership is so powerful.

I can tell you from a hypnosis subject's point of view I live my life healed, whole, happy, and in balanced alignment due to my willingness to create a place and space where the hypnotic triggers and suggestions are allowed to thrive.

Michelle

"That Was Not What I Expected"

From time to time a client epitomizes everything I'm sharing with you, myths and all. During an afternoon weekend class a couple came in. Michelle was visiting from Texas.

Years ago she had experienced a hypnosis session. The retelling of her story was funny and poignant—and truly right on target. The hypnotist had explained to her that she would hear his voice and the expectation of a co-created session with her subconscious. The challenges she faced were severe anorexia and the inability to sleep. Her life was spiraling out of control and she needed help.

He gave her all of the advice I have already mentioned to you. He led her into a comfortable state of relaxation. Michelle said that throughout the entire session she kept thinking, "Well, bless his heart, he thinks this is working, so I will just play along. I don't want to interrupt him by pointing out that I can hear every word he says."

He gave her a treasure trove of solid hypnotic tools and brought her back to the here and now. As she was preparing to leave he reminded her that the sound of his voice would be one way that she could maintain the effects of the suggestions. If she found herself fading back into old habits, she was given a phone number to a recorded line for reinforcement as needed. "Listen to the sound of my voice and as you do, all of your new life changes are powerfully strengthened."

It really is just that simple.

Michelle left his office with the continued thought of "Bless his heart, he thinks that worked" giving her a feeling of peace, calm, and accomplishment.

On her way home this formerly severe anorexic with sleep issues saw a fast food taco place and thought, "Oh wow, I feel hungry." So she pulled to the drive-through and got herself a full meal. Then she ate it… all of it. When she arrived home she was calm and tired so she laid down, not waking until twelve hours later.

The next morning while brushing her teeth, Michelle looked into the mirror and realized, "Holy shit, this stuff works!"

She had gotten exactly what she had asked for. The hypnotist kept it simple and within a platform of partnership. The subtle shift was not apparent until Michelle had eaten and slept for the first time in months.

Often times we as subjects just slip into a new normal. The old challenges and issues are released and the new path is obvious and easy. It is at those times when the effects of hypnosis are gifted into our lives with gentleness at a deep level of awareness.

Michelle said in the coming weeks she not only called and listened to the recording as needed to maintain her life recovery. She also went back and saw him again for more sessions. When she returned it was with the clear knowledge that just because she could hear what he was saying did not mean it wasn't working. Actually the exact opposite became her truth. The positive change she desired became her truth and therefore her new normal.

Patti

"I Knew I Could Fly"

One of the phrases I love to hear when sharing my passion for hypnosis is "I want to have what you're having."

Patti had a unique request we were both excited to explore. She knew that as a small child she could *fly*—she just could not remember the details.

She asked to visit her early childhood skill—through hypnosis—from the depths of her memory. I explained to her the concept of *regression*, visiting past memories with the intention of gaining knowledge and insight to benefit her current life.

The next hour was fascinating. We neither introduced doubt nor assumed an outcome. I escorted Patti back to the time and place and space that as a child she flew.

With a count of 1, then 2, then 3, I asked her if it was day or night.

She said the sun was setting.

I asked if she was inside or outside.

She was outside and it was raining. She was getting wet and did not like it.

I asked if she felt safe and if there were any immediate concerns.

She said she was okay.

The next steps were simple since she was already comfortable and ready.

Patti, from a third-party perspective, was able to watch a car accident she'd experienced as a two-year-old child. She had been a passenger in the back seat of the car her mother was driving. On impact, Patti's little body had been thrown free of the wreck—and she flew through the air— landing safely in a ditch several feet away.

Yep, we had found the moment when, as a child, Patti could fly.

This session taught me a valuable lesson. We carry memories from the viewpoint of the person we were in the moment they happened.

Patti had not remembered clearly until we connected with the two-year-old's perspective. That session also assisted Patti to heal the trauma of that same little girl who watched her mom being rescued, and then couldn't understand why her mom was never quite the same afterward.

Suddenly it all made sense.

Samantha

"Got My Heart Back"

Samantha came to us with a broken heart following a long-term relationship breakup. She was struggling to live her life as a single woman. Samantha had the feeling she would never be whole again.

The stress, strain, and emotional roller coaster were all affecting her day-to-day life. She thought she should feel free, yet instead she felt lost and alone.

Hypnosis is a tremendous tool to work with emotional issues since our subconscious is where emotions live within us. Her memories were raw as she missed the good ones and was experiencing excruciating pain with the bad ones.

She settled in, settled down, and relaxed. Samantha drifted, floated, and dreamed. Then we got started.

She was asked to ponder her boyfriend David and create a picture which would serve as a mental image of their relationship. When she had that picture in mind, we asked her to notice that it was in color. Strong emotional moments are pretty much always remembered in vivid living color.

She was asked to put that picture in a frame of her choice, then write across the front of it, a word or phrase that allowed her to say what she needed to say, freeing herself to place it in her life history museum. At the bottom left corner of the frame was a small drain... a funnel. At the count of 1, then 2, then 3 the color of that picture began to melt, and pool at the bottom. The color drained into Samantha's hand, forming a ball of vivid color. As the color left the frame, the picture transitioned to black and white. The emotions had been neutralized.

Samantha now held the vivid color in her hands, her emotions and memories of David were back within her control. That colored ball began to swirl and with each rotation it gathered momentum and powerful ownership. She was quietly getting her life back—the parts of her she had given away to the relationship.

It was time for them to come back home. The color kept getting brighter as Samantha allowed the magic of healing to consume her brokenness. When that colored ball was as large and as strong as this moment required she lovingly took it in her open hands and placed it into her heart. She welcomed herself home.

The tears fell as she said "Yes" to herself, and reclaimed those parts of her life she had given into the relationship.

When Samantha returned to full awareness a few minutes later, she had a glow in her eyes that relayed freedom from the prison she'd been in before. She had lost something precious and was welcoming it home.

Hypnosis allowed her the gift to reclaim what she had invested in a relationship which didn't work out. She received *herself* back, and then felt free to go forth into a fresh new life in possession of 100% of who she was… safe and sound.

Nicole

"Monsters in the Closet"

A staggeringly high number of women in our society have experienced some level of inappropriate sexual contact before the age of full consent.

It is never a surprise when a phrase such as, "He should not have been touching me that way," is spoken in my office. Many of these memories have been held by Subconscious within a closed protected area. When someone is finally ready to deal with a life issue such as self-esteem, anxiety, weight loss, etc., it sometimes becomes apparent during hypnosis that the root of their issue returns them to a moment where they felt powerless, controlled by someone else—and not in a good way.

Nicole came to us with numerous issues and life challenges. Everything seemed to be elaborately protected by her subconscious and she could only proceed when she felt absolutely safe. She did not seem to have the ability to live casual or carefree. Everything was a crisis; drama ruled her days while fear ruled her nights.

In essence she was a hot mess.

Her desire was to feel safe in her own skin again. She was tired of feeling like she could not adequately take care of herself. She was smart, and strong, she was dedicated and determined. Yet from her perspective she felt violated from within.

She came to us for multiple sessions. One issue hid another. Ultimately we decided to begin by addressing her concern, "I am having trouble sleeping."

Once she was assured within herself and securely partnered with her subconscious, we began the necessary deep healing.

Nicole had experienced rape as a young woman. She was violated, and due to her perception of her situation, did not tell anyone. Decades later, she was finally willing to open the necessary doors to neutralize the damage caused by those events.

Hypnosis allowed her to hypnotically confront her attacker; this time she was in control. Subconscious had held those memories secure for a reason and the flow of information was not available upon our request... but rather at whatever pace she could handle.

She was also dealing with guilt that on the night of the rape she had been drunk. Compound that with more guilt, because after that night she stayed drunk for years.

Forgiveness is key for recovery and healing. "To let go of the things you cannot change" had been her mantra and kept her sober for nearly 20 years at the time we met her. That phrase took on new meaning when she began to release her pent-up attempts to unsuccessfully hold her life together.

One session was spent saving a child who sat on her bed terrified of the monster in the closet. We turned the light on and told the monster he was no longer allowed to stay. He was invited to leave. That memory faded to black and white. We cleaned out the closet. No more monsters.

Hypnosis is an effective tool when invited to create a safe place of healing, even from the most traumatic incidents that life throws at us.

Sexual health and well-being is one area that when partnered with hypnosis, can bring about true freedom. The magic is in that the healing is personal for each individual. Sometimes sexual well-being is not a monster in the closet. Regardless of the cause, the effect of hypnosis can and will set you free.

Tammy

"Goodbye, Dad"

The blurry years came into focus.

Tammy had been fascinated by the concept and the possibilities of hypnosis and when her timing allows she joins us in our Maryland office for classes and other hypnotic events. We worked with her mom, for weight loss. It turned into a session dedicated to the death of her husband a few years before. Grief had manifested in the form of a few extra pounds. Her mom was a clear example that the presenting issue is often not the root of the problem.

Tammy sat next to her mother, having no clue that her own grief was about to overwhelm her. She felt the gut-wrenching loss of her dad.

After her mom's session she and I talked about a realization she had eight years of her life holding no active memories. Not amnesia, but more a case of living them did not require being recorded. They were some of her formative years and she turned out okay so they must not be important.

Tammy shared one of the things that bothered her most was that she did not have a chance to say goodbye to her dad. He went into surgery and did not return. There was a hole in her heart that had been there since the day he died.

Count 1, then 2, then 3… remember a time when you were a kid… when you and your dad were together and having fun.

She went back to a day when her dad was teaching her about taking pictures. Her awareness perked up. "Oh God," she said, "my Dad gave me his love for photography." Tammy is an amazing photographer, and now the deeper roots of that skill were revealed.

Fast forward to the hospital room, before her father's surgery. Adult Tammy now knows she was telling him goodbye. The bittersweet farewell was filled with tears and the gift of undying love for her dad. More importantly she experienced the love which poured from her dad back to her. He told her he would be with her always and would never forget the love they share.

Tammy was set free from that burden of, "I did not get to tell him goodbye." A broken piece began to heal.

She was able to sit down with the spirit of her dad and tell him about her life. She shared her hopes and her dreams, she shared her challenges and her fears. Tammy pulled out an array of photos to show her dad. From beneath his pillow he pulled an even bigger album. He had been watching over her since the day he left and cataloged and kept every picture she had ever taken.

Then he told her his secret.

'Look at the pictures, Precious. I am with you,' she heard his voice say. *'Look for me as the glint on the water and the sparkle in the sky. I taught you how to frame your shots, I taught you to play with the lighting and I have stayed with you, steadying your hand while helping you create your pictures and your business.'*

"Dad," Tammy replied. "The name of my business is Shooting Stars."

He answered simply, *'I know, baby. Now go look at your pics.'* Since that day she finds the sparkle, the glint, that small wink of dad in her photos and does not miss him with a grieving heart any longer.

That session had no time limit so Tammy just stayed and talked with her dad for a long time. Hypnosis allows for such things because if you can imagine it you can have a relationship with it. That night on her way home she stopped at the bridge near her house, brought out her camera, and (feeling her dad with her) she took the most magnificent picture of a moon beam glistening off the creek bed.

Would he be with her always? Absolutely. She was willing for that to be her truth, so he meets her there always.

The missing years returned as well, and as expected, she had not missed much. Except her Dad. A kid in recovery does not have to remember every little thing. Our subconscious is totally ready, willing and able to carry the memories and emotions when our thinking mind cannot bear the weight.

Hope vs. Marty

"New Normal or NOT?"

From a subject's point of view, the major gift of hypnosis is the myriad of choice and possibility. Nothing is ever forced with a 100% consensual partnership between what is possible and what you choose to accept or reject.

We have learned in multiple situations that truth is truth, if it's truth for ME.

A group of people could experience the same hypnotic session. One might walk away forever changed—profoundly set free upon a path for restoration, growth, healing—and the other could walk away thinking, "This is total bullshit." Others still could decide to receive the change, take it out for a test-drive to see how it fits and feels before making an informed decision.

All are valid choices, but as you may have guessed, it works best to opt for the "This is awesome" route.

I am rarely disappointed.

Hope and Marty are examples of the far ends of this spectrum.

Marty is a D.C. businessman who dedicated his life to public service. He is strong, smart, capable, and respected. After years of service he became curious about the possibilities of relaxing from his rigorous schedule, but didn't have a clue how to begin to let go of his high profile, fast-paced life.

Hope's life took a devastating turn when her husband of many years came home one day to inform her he would be filing for divorce. It was not even a discussion; her marriage was just over. This news put her health challenges and physical symptoms into overdrive.

Both of these dear hearts became long-term clients, working through one issue then another… some easier than others.

It did not take long before the shifts and changes of hypnosis motivated positive change within them both. These changes in turn created within them a "new normal."

When you look at something differently, what you are looking at changes.

This is reframing at its best.

For both of them it became a quest of, "If I am not who I've always been, then who am I?"

Both had partnered with their subconscious. Both made decisions to walk into their new life with confidence. Yet both had a decision to make to continue that new life.

When prior limiting beliefs are removed, it can get tricky to find a new path and stay on it long enough for all new habits to form.

Choices and possibilities for a fresh perspective are ahead of you, but if you spend too much time looking in the rear view mirror, it will be difficult to navigate the road ahead.

Hope had been pain-free for quite some time thanks to hypnosis and her partnership with her subconscious, but her "new normal" found her craving the familiar. The pain of divorce and the physical pain which followed had been faithful companions, loyal to her for many years. As she faced a future of change and possibility, she instead chose the comfort of retrieving that blanket of pain which would not leave her.

Yes, the pain returned.

On the one hand she was devastated the pain had returned, yet it was comforting to have her old friend back again. Her opinion was that the hypnosis had not actually "worked." She returned to her previous normal, and life moved on. She now doubts hypnosis as a successful tool for her life issues, and that has become her truth.

We wish her well. She is a perfect example that hypnosis is a pathway to powerful transformation at the mind level. But changing our mind has always, and always will be, a choice.

Marty began to see his world with fresh eyes. He realized his stress could be significantly minimized by focusing on and maintaining his intentions of building a new normal for his life.

The partnership with his subconscious included a continuous willingness to be open and ready to share a fresh perspective from within. As his new normal came into focus, he just kept expanding the relaxations, and asking his inner self to assist him to let go of the years of bureaucracy cataloged within his system.

Stress was invited to relax, anxiety invited to ease, and he filled himself with a continued peace.

He chose for this low-stress "new normal" (offered by hypnosis and the partnership with his subconscious) to become his fresh lifestyle. He continues to thrive within it.

What's the Difference?

What's the difference between these two stories? A hypnotist would give you all sorts of explanations and suggestions, but from the subject's perspective, I will say that life is filled with choices.

Even when "new normal" is spectacular, it is still one or more steps away from the dependence you had on "what used to be."

There is an adjustment to "new normal." It takes practice to let old habits, roles, relationships, and limitations go. To release them and walk fully into the place and space where they are either gone or seriously realigned takes courage. And practice!

Doug

"I Got My Music Back"

Deep trance is a phenomenal escorted journey into the core center of body and mind healing. It is the center from which natural healing occurs on a continual basis.

I met Doug at a weekend festival. He was a free spirit and ready to check out what hypnosis had to offer. We had a session pre-talk, but as you will soon realize, much was left unsaid before we began.

Shortly after the session started, I felt a deep sadness within Doug.

I told him that if he was willing to push it out—to release that sadness—on the count of 3, I would pull with everything I had. I would take nothing from him, but instead I would partner with him to release whatever was troubling him.

I began to count, and as I did he began to push out that silent sadness. Since I am a very visual person I can often imagine scenes in video quality. I explained to him that I saw a bubble rising up and out of his chest. A hot air balloon of sorts, attached to the sadness, very respectfully carried it way.

It was obvious that Doug was experiencing something profound.

I continued to count as the sadness lifted and was carried away. A moment later I could see a bright light being poured into the hole which remained—as if from a waterfall. It felt loving and healing; it looked bright and golden.

Somewhere during this time Doug started to cry. Initially, tears of pain and pressure morphed into tears of release and relief.

Please realize at this point I did not know Doug beyond our few minutes' meeting. I had no knowledge of his life or personal struggles.

He simply saw our hypnosis booth and thought, "Hey, I wanna give this a try."

When Doug was brought back to awareness, it was obvious he would need a moment to compose himself and adjust to the newness of what had just happened.

He looked at me and said, "Oh my God, pretty lady, you just gave me my music back."

He was both surprised and ecstatic to have found an old and rich friend which had been missing. We did not talk much about his music at this point, but it was obvious he was thrilled to have it back. It seemed that his music had never left him, but had been covered up by the sadness. Without the weight of that pain, his music could resurface.

As you might suspect, there is always more to a story—and Doug's is a big one.

Doug had been a professional musician, with a passion for his craft. He worked night shift at the AT&T building in what is now respectfully known as Ground Zero in New York City.

In the early morning of September 11, 2001, Doug had just stepped out into the morning light when he saw the first plane hit the twin towers.

Throughout the moments that followed he watched the events of that horrible day unfold right before his eyes. When the first tower collapsed he was standing on the roof of his building, with a clear knowledge that death was coming for him and he was about to be crushed.

Yet for reasons he could not possibly comprehend, he lived and did not die. His building had the only undamaged generators in that quadrant of the city. Within a short period of time, the AT&T building became the generated power source for the response efforts.

Doug did not go home for 28 days. He stayed there keeping those generators up and running.

During that month though, he did take the time to attend 56 funerals for his friends—firefighters he knew from the local hangout.

When we met Doug the 9/11 disaster had been 10 years before, yet was still vividly fresh for him.

He had not picked up his guitar since that fateful day, and as far as he could tell, his music died when the towers fell.

I knew none of this story during that initial session. The sadness that lifted, he would explain in the coming months, was that core level pain and anguish that had been locked in. In the moment he looked at me and said, "Pretty lady, you've just given me my music back," he felt his life could—and would—finally begin again.

Doug's good friend Kris had known him for three years. She said his guitar case was covered with dust in the corner, untouched for the entire time she had known him. She did not even know he knew how to play it.

When he began playing again, Doug had a fresh outlook on life. He felt like a new man.

We stayed in touch and a few months later we had another opportunity to get back together. Kris and I had a heart to heart and she told me that every year on September 11, Doug went through a gut-wrenching traumatic reliving of the events. She asked if we would be willing to help him before he had to go through it again in just a few days.

We agreed to meet, to set our intentions for Doug's highest interests. None of us expected it to be easy, however we all expected success.

Doug and Kris settled together in a comfortable space as Larry placed Doug into trance. He went deeply, now a comfortable hypnosis participant.

Larry started by asking Doug to take a snapshot of his memories… to place them in a frame… and then fade them to black and white.

Larry hypnotically handed Doug a gold pen with which he wrote "Never Forget" onto each photo. Larry told him that he did not have to forget to heal; he just needed to place the pictures on the wall behind him, so that when he chose to turn around and look at them they would always be there.

Behind him. No longer in front of him all the time.

Doug asked for a swivel chair so he could spin quickly if necessary.

Fair enough. The chair spins. Done!

Then we began the process of Doug gathering up the grief and emotions that the mere thought of 9/11 created within him.

He started to cry. Larry assured him we were not going to stop or stay. We were only going in long enough to gather what needed to be released.

As the bubble of Doug's personal experience built, Larry kept assuring him he was doing great. I had my hand on his shoulder and Kris held him in her arms as he sobbed on with the intensity of those moments.

Then Larry said, "Okay, Doug, I am going to count from one to three, and as I count, the intensity will build with the expectation of this releasing from you."

Although crying, Doug shook his head yes, and authorized Larry to continue.

"At 3, let it build. All that needs to go, allow it to gather, 2, stronger still," and as Larry got to "1," Doug screamed, *"They were my friends!"*

The anguish, terror, and grief flowed out and away from him, as if a pressurized pipe had burst.

He held my hand, he grabbed onto Kris, and he followed every suggestion Larry poured into his wounded heart. Doug's entire being was releasing and healing quickly.

Larry led him to focus on whatever memory or event presented itself into his thoughts. With the assistance of his subconscious, those thoughts, memories, and emotions became bubbles. All he needed do was put them in his hands and then pop the bubble.

Our friend laid there and popped bubbles. The flood gates had been opened, the bubbles popped and he was going to be okay.

We spent time inviting those places and spaces that had been released to heal fully. To heal completely. To heal absolutely for Doug's greatest good.

That year 9/11 was only a few days away. Doug was both calm and subdued during the memorial day. He remembered with the utmost respect, yet was not anguished by those memories, nor did he have to watch it all on TV like he previously felt he had to.

The 9/11s since have all been somber, while Doug continues to be free of the burdens he chose to release that day.

His healing was from the core of his heart and as such he soars.

In the years since we started working together, Doug has become a certified hypnotist, and also plays his music regularly. What began as open mic night at various bars and clubs morphed into him playing four nights a week with his new band.

Part of his recovery included starting to write music. He composed and dedicated a song to me called, "My Beautiful Amazing Grace," which he plays at every performance.

Our friendship began with me wanting to share what I had learned. He was a stranger who said, "Sure, what the hell. I'll give it a try."

Now he is a dear friend who lives in the music. If you ask him he will tell you...

> *I am the music,*
> *and the music is me.*
> *Let it be.*

Let it be.

Self-hypnosis

When talking about self-hypnosis there is a huge difference between answering the questions "What is it?" and "How do I do it?"

There are many reasons for knowing how to incorporate self-hypnosis into your life to establish a point of inner balance.

As I have shared from my heart, the opportunity to partner with that part of you who takes care of 50 million things a day (most of which you will never even know or acknowledge) is priceless.

To have a working relationship with your habit former, your inner personal image, the keeper of your memories, your pathfinder… is huge. When I met my subconscious my life transformed.

I am unique and I love it that way, however getting to know your subconscious is something each of us can do. We can and do already have that connection, but your subconscious is eager to join you in a more recognizable way along the journey.

How?

We actually all go into self-inspired hypnosis multiple times every day.

How many times have you driven somewhere without consciously noting all the turns along the way? You reach your destination with at least a portion of the trip unaccounted for in your upfront thinking mind. You were not asleep, nor inattentive; you simply allowed your mind to drift for the journey.

Your subconscious is an excellent driver. She is the one who helped establish the skill in the first place.

Now imagine that same trip, but with traffic or bad weather. Your focus is single-minded. Your every intention is on the road immediately ahead. Your subconscious pulls out a list of additional things for you to pay attention to for your safety.

I have never been more tranced while driving than the cold rainy night in the Pocono Mountains where the only thing I could see clearly was the back of the tractor trailer in front of me. I knew if I focused on, and stayed in his tracks, I would make it through the mountain pass. Afterward I was exhausted from the concentration.

How many times have you read a good book and not looked up for fifty or even a hundred pages? During that time you had seen, heard, felt, and embraced life through one or more characters… as deeply and intimately as if you'd lived it yourself. That page break which brought you back to reality was probably prompted by a need to go to the bathroom or turn on a lamp.

Or maybe you were watching a TV show or movie and became so immersed you were practically a member of the cast. Your heart races right along with the heroes, you feel what they feel, you share their highs and lows. Then in the blink of your eye, a commercial jerks you back to the reality of the room you are seated in. That return to the here and now can be quite jarring.

You lay down to sleep, knowing that as you sleep you will dream. Knowing that the dreams you dream are important even if you do not remember them. Know that your day is being settled in your mind, and it is time to give your subconscious whatever time is needed to put everything away to get ready for your next waking moment.

Your subconscious is continual, she watches over you as your conscious mind sleeps. That is her time to set habits within you, it is her time to sort out the memories and or shut down the momentum of your day.

Emotions are invited to rest, points of view are invited to settle, and dreams are invited to create choices and possibilities.

It is said that the last significant thought you have before drifting off to sleep will carry you through the night and will be with you as you awaken. So make it a positive one.

Who do you think gives you the options as you sift through your day for significance? That's right. *Thank you, Subconscious.*

How many times have you faced a challenge that required all your concentration? All you need do is take a deep breath, and allow what you know to rise to the surface. *Thank you, Subconscious.*

As I said all of us go into self-hypnosis multiple times a day, anytime our conscious thinking mind needs a break or some extra help.

Then there are those magical moments when we *choose*, we decide, we ask our subconscious to join us on our journey with meaningful and active participation. That is where the good stuff lives. When we take a moment to breathe in… breathe out… and simply say, "Subconscious, I could really use your help."

The easiest way to set yourself up for success is to expect it will work.

Two of the first questions we ask when working with a hypnosis client is, "Do you want this to work?" and "Do you desire to be successfully hypnotized?"

If the answer to both questions is yes then you have already won.

Your subconscious is ready, willing and able to step into a partnership role with you. Begin by asking yourself, would I like to take this moment to partner with my subconscious?

For a moment allow me to assume you would like to return to a memory—to feel as if you were right back there again.

You can choose to return there as merely an observer or to step in as an active participant.

Imagine a childhood birthday party. Who was there? What gifts did you get? What flavor was your cake? As you step into that memory you have the ability to fully experience it again.

Once you have chosen the memory you desire to visit, settle in… settle down… relax. Ask Subconscious to transport you to that time, place and space.

While she is pulling it all together for you, believe it is possible. Then when she has it ready, step into it fully. You may get a quick glimpse or you may stay for a while.

You may see, feel, or realize things you had long since forgotten. Then is when you come to realize that your subconscious *has not forgotten.* The more you open to the memory the more she pours.

This is a fabulous place from which to let go of resentments or aggravations. Look into that memory and invite the challenge to release… to dissolve… and let go.

It's a memory anyway, so who need to hold onto the crappy parts?

If your life would be better if you chose to forgive, then do it!

Forgive and step into the freedom from the other side.

For a moment allow yourself to focus on a memory of something which required your complete attention. As you feel the need for a break or fresh inspiration, it's yours. Invite Subconscious into your moment. Take a deep breath… ask for guidance… ask for peace… ask for inner knowledge to come forth. As you relax into knowing you are no longer expected to juggle the weight of the situation alone you can begin to unwind. The burden gets lighter.

Breathe in imagination… breathe out imagination.

Breathe in awareness... breathe out awareness.

Breathe in clarity... breathe out clarity.

As you release the tightly wound spring, like magic your relaxation level rises even though your circumstance is still there.

Request a fresh perspective, knowing that when you look at something differently, what you are looking at changes.

That is such a powerful truth. And it can be yours. Yours to use as frequently as you need.

Self-hypnosis taps into the very heart of who you are. Your subconscious knows all the same people as you and she might give you a nudge to ask for assistance from someone you had not realized could shift the balance of this challenge. She also might remind you of a silly joke when what you really need is to smile right about now.

There are tons of tools and techniques for self-hypnosis.

1. When you desire to concentrate on something specific, put your thumb and forefinger together and ask Subconscious to enhance your thought and to take you there.
2. Listen to a recording with an openness to receive the message being spoken.
3. Meditate, being open to Subconscious joining you.
4. Ask yourself a question and then be willing to take action on the choices and possibilities presented to you.

Practice self-hypnosis continually and your life will be better for it.

I would honestly recommend going to visit a good, solid hypnotist who can guide you through these first few steps. Having a great initial experience will set you up for maximum success, and give you important resources.

For the tough stuff, for the therapy needs, please make a session appointment and speak to someone, who like Larry or me, has a toolbox as big as their heart, combined with the willingness to be your guide, your escort while you create within yourself positive change.

You are not expected to figure it all out by yourself. You can however truly enjoy playing around with whatever you find works best for you. The journey is as great as the destination.

Popping Bubbles

Our lives, the world we live in, and everything around us is constantly shifting, changing, and evolving. That is the magic and beauty of life. We have the opportunity to make choices every day.

One of the awesome things about hypnosis is that when we invite our subconscious to partner with us, for our best and highest interests, she will open up levels of awareness, knowledge, and understanding that allow for a new life to emerge.

I have had the time to develop skills with many hypnotic tools and techniques which helped build the new habits of my life. They are now tools I do not have to think about or even recognize. I just trust my subconscious to handle things for me, which she has always done. That has been her job, after all, even before we were formally introduced through hypnosis.

My subconscious and I developed a way to "gamify" hypnosis.

We came to realize the power of popping bubbles.

Think for a moment of something that truly irritates you, something that would make your life much more fun if it were to diminish.

Now imagine a bubble that can and will easily swallow up that item. The bubble, with the assistance of your subconscious, grows bigger, bigger, and even bigger. As the bubble grows, you begin to realize that the irritant seems smaller, and smaller, and smaller. It looks and seems so insignificant inside this special bubble.

This bubble is personally designed to diminish all things that are taking up too much space in your current situation.

With the finesse of a small child chasing a wayward floating bubble on a summer's day, reach up... wrap your intentions around that bubble... and POP that sucker.

The contents of your bubble have now been obliterated. You notice that the issue which was within is now in a million shattered pieces. Gone. Released in a way that allows you to let it go. There is nothing left to hold onto.

Now the flip side.

Think of a moment or a relationship... or something that is close to your heart... something that defines your life as fun and happy... something that just makes you feel good.

Now place that "thought" into an all-encompassing bubble.

As before, the bubble grows at an immense rate and is now enormous. However this time, instead of the contents diminishing, they grow along with the space and size and scope of the bubble. Regardless of how big the bubble gets, the item within it gives you that much more joy.

Now race with the wind... reach up... and pop your bubble.

As it blasts into the world around you, realize that this feeling... this moment... this event... the way it makes you feel... is literally everywhere. You can see it, feel it, taste it, and you know that it will be forever free.

My husband and I have spent a great deal of time laying in each other's arms and popping bubbles for every question we could think of. Then one day we quit defining the issues as good or bad. We realized that in every moment there is contrast. Instead, we have started to put our content into a bubble and ask our subconscious to grow what's needed to grow… and shrink what's needed to be shrunk. And then we popped… popped… popped.

Later we even quit placing specific thoughts or issues within our bubbles. We began asking our subconscious to just simply choose for us. We now reach into the sky for unseen, undefined bubbles and when they pop we always feel the freedom.

Burnin' Down the House

Life goes on and on and on.

One Sunday afternoon in March 2014, my phone rang. I did not recognize the number, so I assumed it was a miss-dial or something equally unimportant. I was wrong.

It was my neighbor across the street saying, "Sondra, honey, your house is on fire."

I said, "Okay."

"No, darling. This is serious. There are five fire trucks here and your house is engulfed in flames right now."

In that instant I forgot I had just talked to Larry at our office. I started to scream into the phone, "Is Larry in there? Oh my God, is Larry okay?"

She told me his car was not in the driveway.

I calmed down.

This is by definition one of those moments when the life I thought I had a grip on was ripped away and shattered into a million pieces.

I was 20 minutes from home with groceries in the car. There was very little I could "do."

I called Larry and told him to meet me at the house because it was on fire. Our daughter Rachel was with her dad at the office. She turned on her smartphone and (as an executive producer for ABC news) saw numerous news alerts of a house on fire in Bowie. She looked into the southern sky and saw a huge black smoke cloud.

"Dad, this is serious. I can see the smoke from here."

The distance between the house and the office is about eight miles.

I called several people during that 20-minute drive then pulled up to the police barricade that had our entire neighborhood blocked off. I rolled down my window and simply said, "I have been informed that it is my house on fire."

"Follow me, ma'am."

There was this weird numb feeling as I walked the block from the car to the place I had considered my home for nearly 17 years, with firefighters, hoses, trucks, and responders literally everywhere.

The tower truck doused the smoldering ruins with a steady stream of water blasting into my bedroom through the open space that used to be a roof and ceiling. There were still active flames in the garage and the front porch roof. Men with axes, wearing air tanks. Water everywhere. My yard was a sea of mud, filled with the footprints of 50 sets of responders' boots.

The strangest assortment of things—that would have been considered personal when I left the house at 8 am—were now very publicly covering the driveway, the yard, and showing through the gaping holes in what used to be my house.

The media showed up. Our daughter Rachel went to them and asked for professional courtesy, and they gave us great respect. Across the street was a line of guys hoping we would hire them on the spot to assist with the rebuild. They kept sneaking across the police line to hand me things like a toothbrush, a stuffed animal, or a folder of information.

I was safe, no one was injured and my beloved was okay. Larry and I were told later it was an "eight-minute fire." From the time it started until the house was consumed in the inferno, it took only eight minutes.

It is at a moment such as this when the years of living with and loving a hypnotist really paid off.

I maintained a feeling of calm and ease that did not require explanation. There was nothing we could do to reverse the day. Living in the present moment was never more clear.

I stood in my driveway and realized I was the best dressed woman there. But the clothes on my back were literally all I owned.

This dress, this coat, these shoes. That was it.

My subconscious takes care of me all day, everyday, and that was never more true than the day my house burnt down.

She held me close and kept a check on my emotions and responses to the strangest things. When we got the all-clear, my son Bryan put his arm around my shoulder, and walked with me to the back of the house. We took a deep breath together. The back slider door had been obliterated and glass was everywhere.

Bryan said he wished he had been the one to destroy that door… it had never worked well.

Humor helped. It always does.

The walk-through—although shocking—was not devastating. Everything we owned had been destroyed, yet there was nothing I could think of that held any importance. The walls were gone, the roof was gone, and everything was dripping. The floor held a couple inches of water.

My thoughts were silly like, "Well, that doesn't belong there," or "Oh God, what a mess."

Our best friends pulled up soon afterward. They had driven 90 minutes, under threat of an upcoming snow storm. They did not care about the weather, they cared about us. I walked into open arms and just simply said, "Dwayne, my house just burned down."

He replied in his Louisiana drawl, "I know, darlin'."

At that moment I needed nothing more than his hug.

My son Bryan took us to his home which was not far away. I was met at the door by my eight-year-old grandson who gave me another hug.

"Nana, I know you are sad that your house burned down, so I will be sad with you."

"Thank you, buddy," I said.

Sitting around the dining room table celebrating life, we realized that on a scale of "1 to 10" this day was only a "2" compared to the night back in 1995 when our son Nick suffered a massive stroke.

Hands down, this was a piece of cake.

The shock had begun to wear off.

We were all safe.

We were together.

We could face the next steps later.

In that present moment we decided to celebrate family. It was as simple as taking a deep breath, and pouring a glass of Gentleman Jack.

Settle in… settle down… and relax.

Everything was going to be okay.

I Grieved My Toothbrush

Ten months after we stood in our driveway and watched our material possessions go up in flames, Larry and I were still handling the twists, turns, and issues of recovery.

There is no doubt the hypnosis we shared at every step of the journey carried us through.

That week's project was debris removal. Three guys with big black trash bags had been working for days in 32-degree weather.

I went to our rental house and picked up a crochet project I had recently started. I was feeling kinda low, but felt better when I touched the blanket and got into the repetition of the sameness of the craft.

Crocheting is a perfect self-hypnosis tool. You focus on the hook, you watch the yarn flow. There is nothing to concentrate on at all. You are free to just drift, float, and dream.

After a couple hours of mindless blanket magic I went to bed.

In the morning Larry asked if I was feeling better. I tried to explain that I was fine, nothing was wrong, and all was good. On and on.

I told him that for ten months I had been okay about what happened to our house. We didn't lose anything that was truly important. The shock was well past.

Then I started to cry.

I cried over the black bags which were carrying the debris of 17 years of my life. I cried that they were being put into a dumpster to be hauled away as garbage.

I laid there sobbing for my toothbrush.

I honestly don't even remember what color it was.

I cried for the clean dishes in the dishwasher.

And I cried for my broom.

Larry held me in his arms and whispered, "Drop, baby. It's going to be okay."

The hypnosis that morning was so tender, so loving, and so intimate.

Larry spoke to my subconscious and all that was within me, asking what I was feeling. He held me while my broken heart cried for perceived loss, knowing that healing was on its way.

From within the cocoon of loving healing hypnosis, I cried the tears of a woman who knew how to release stress and anxiety. I was relieved to be able to go with the natural flow, not holding onto the crap.

Within a few minutes it was apparent we were in a shared trance, and were dealing with the next phase of our lives together. We were in a conversational hypnotic experience, partnered on a subconscious level.

When we finished, I opened my eyes. His face was right above mine. I reached up to wipe my tears and realized he had tears as well. Since I was already there, I wiped his cheeks, too.

Sometimes hypnosis is not a formal session with a beginning, middle, and end. Sometimes it is allowing your subconscious to take the front position and share what is happening from within. Sometimes it is okay to not have an agenda, but rather an open heart to receive, and open ears to hear what the very core of you has to say.

And when you finish, you wipe your tears and go on with your day.

I drove by the house and the first dumpster was filled to the max. Much of the downstairs was empty to the floors. The walls and ceiling boards were gone as well.

I wouldn't grieve my toothbrush for long. I actually felt much better already.

Hypnosis has the ability to soothe me like nothing else. It reaches deeper, heals smoother, and has a resonance that rings true every time.

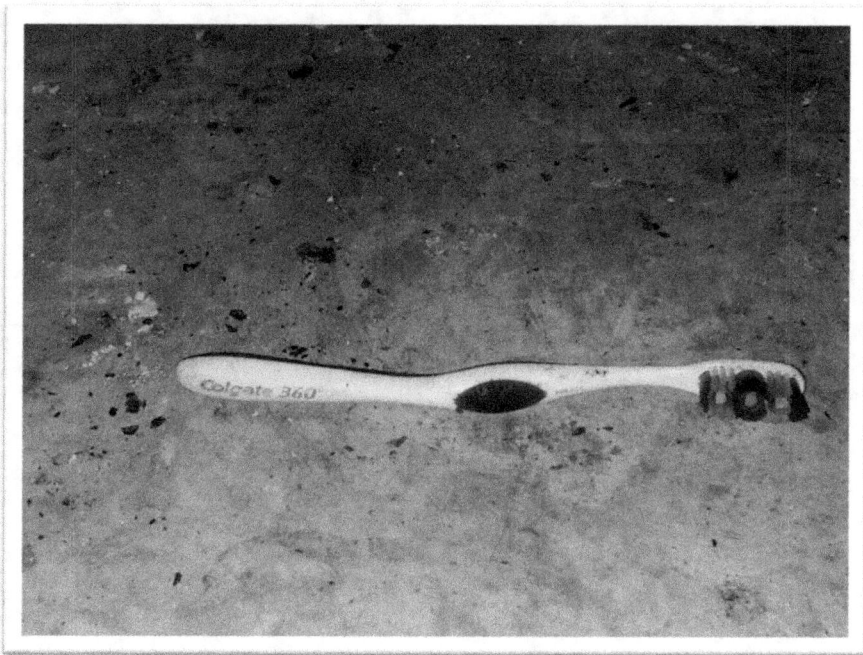

Play Ball

There are many hypnotic tools which can take the "sting" out of things in life that bite us.

I am not sure how I would have balanced everything without the magical layers of hypnosis we used in the days, weeks, and months surrounding the fire.

After taking such a long time to sift through the rubble to find anything we chose to carry out, I assumed I was going to be okay. We would "get on with our lives."

I had been overwhelmed that first day of rubble removal and got all emotional. It was not that I wanted or needed anything still inside, but rather the harsh reality that everything I owned fit in a dumpster. Everything I owned could be taken out in black plastic bags, thrown in the trash, and hauled away on the back of a garbage truck.

A couple of days later we were laying in bed talking about all the changes and how things were finally moving quickly. I got emotional. The sadness of perceived loss gave me another hug and I chose to hug her back.

I heard her message. "This is a process, a flow. As we go through this together, healing and freshness are not only possible, but *promised*."

As expected Larry softly said, "Sleep now, baby. I've got you." I dropped easily into hypnotic trance under the voice and guidance of my beloved.

He called out my subconscious, and asked her how she was doing, She said that Sondra was sad but overall doing okay. He asked her what would help at that present moment and she said it would be nice to go over to the house and realize that not all was lost.

"Okay, Subconscious. Let's go there now. Be in the house." He snapped his fingers.

I was standing in the empty dining room with most of the rubble gone, along with the wall boards and ceiling.

Then he asked, "Okay, honey. Tell me what is still here."

Like magic, I realized my memories were still there. The emotions that were born and nurtured were still there. The habits were still there. The fire did not destroy the core of our home. It only burnt off the house, not our home.

"Okay, Subconscious. I want you to take those things that are still there and collect them into something beautiful."

As I stood in the center of my dining room, things unseen began to form into shiny, glowing floating balls. At the speed of thought the house was lit and filled with these floating spheres of what was *real*, of what was still ours. Untouched by flames or flood, there was true magic.

As the spheres formed and floated around, my subconscious suggested we play ball in the house.

What a surprise, I had a baseball bat in my hands! With the balls of light and love floating all around, there was no concern of knocking over a lamp or breaking a window. There were none of those around. We played baseball in the house for quite some time… laughing, running, shouting, and sharing our hearts in a place I had thought on some level was lost.

It was whimsical, and fun, and refreshing. The more we played with the floating lit balls, the more they glowed, and our love for the life we shared in that house was mixed with the promise of what was being created.

As we played ball in the house, I healed a bit more and another broken piece of me came home.

Hello, Subconscious —
Make It So

A door has been opened for you to build a significant connection with your subconscious.

However does any of this really matter if you don't know how to communicate? Unless you figure out what works for you on a personal level, then this is all just someone else's great story of a fabulous experience.

There are many different modes of communications available, but for today we are discussing hypnosis as the bridge.

Take the time to find what works best for you, then build upon that. Once you open communications the creative avenues that present themselves will come in ways yet to be discovered. You will no longer have to rely on what you know and understand right here and right now. The relationship you will build will be unique.

The authentic nature of that intimacy is yours and yours alone.

If you are struggling for a simple phrase, or a thought to help you begin, I offer:

"Hello, Subconscious. Make it So."

Subconscious holds, guards, and protects your innermost knowledge, awareness, clarity, and wisdom. She has the willingness to hold everything in a balanced position of alignment.

If we were to consider our lives as pieces of a puzzle, Subconscious would be the container they all fit within. Sometimes the pieces are jumbled up. It may take time and space to lay them out to get the right pieces in the right places.

Some pieces may be upside down. Until they are flipped over in the light of day, and *seen*, we have no clue where they will fit best.

On an easy day our lives are a 50-piece puzzle. Other times it's 1,000 pieces with no discernible border.

Yet Subconscious holds them all—large or small—regardless of the moment imprinted upon them.

Together you become masters of the puzzle. The more time spent, the smoother the communications and the stronger the bonds.

When I watch my grandkids put a puzzle together that they have played with many times before it is a quick and easy process.

They simply "Make it so."

Hypnosis assists you to meet and then build a meaningful connection with your subconscious. The "Make it so" concept was one of the earliest tools given to me as a hypnotic subject. Conversations within hypnosis are the initial connections built with an intention for continued use. What is first a path becomes a road, which becomes a highway, which later becomes a jet trail. Wider… then higher… then faster.

But it all begins with "Hello, Subconscious."

The beginnings of any relationship should be built carefully. This one is no exception. Get acquainted, and get comfortable. Build what we in the hypnosis community call *rapport*.

When you can feel what the other feels, and things shift at the speed of thought, you will be able to finish each other's sentences because you are just that connected.

For me, I built communications skills while driving home from D.C. every workday afternoon for over a year. I asked my inner self to meet me in my dreams, and I still maintain regular hypnosis sessions where I am in trance and my hypnotist is guiding the discussions and explorations. I talk with my subconscious as my true ally and friend.

Once the partnership has been established, and the connection is strong, you will find an active state of relaxed trance is no longer necessary to create and enrich your life. While being fully awake and alert, you can ask your subconscious for help, then say, "Make it so." Allow your subconscious to do what she does best. She loves simple instructions and wants nothing more than to intimately connect with you in a day to day, moment by moment relationship.

I desire to see something good in this situation ~ Make it so.

Help me focus on the task at hand ~ Make it so.

Where did I leave my keys? ~ Make it so.

I'm chilled. Will you warm me up, please? ~ Make it so.

I am so tired. I ask for you to calm my thoughts and slide me off to sleep. ~ Make it so.

I do not feel well. Do I need medical assistance? ~ Make it so.

The stress of this moment is not cool, calm me down. ~ Make it so.

I want to remember the good times. ~ Make it so.

I need fresh perspective. ~ Make it so.

When the relationship between you and your hypnotist is one of earned trust and you know you are safe, there is nothing better than to give your hypnotist permission to utilize the "Make it so" phrase, both in person and remotely.

Traditional trance will no longer be necessary when the agreement between Subconscious and your hypnotist or guide has been reached. Subconscious will listen to the sound of their voice in its various forms, and follow simple instructions.

The partnership builds momentum for your highest and greatest good. Since Subconscious has the "job" of taking care of you all the way down to the core level, any and all suggestions are filtered, then followed.

There have been times when I was stressed about something and Larry will simply say, "Calm her down. Make it so." Subconscious follows the instructions perfectly. She prefers simple instructions. They allow her to create positive change in all the right places. Perhaps calm at that moment is a cup of tea, or a walk, or a nap, or a call with a friend, or even a good cry.

The point of this chapter is to say that none of this matters if you do not connect with the part of you that takes care of you 24/7. Healing, wholeness, life repair, exploration, and discovery of fresh beginnings, all begin with the simple willingness to allow your subconscious to "Make it so."

Scripts, Tools & Terms

Please note that these are tools that have been useful to me as a hypnotic subject. They are also tools which can be used by a hypnotist to become an effective escort or guide. Some of them are both. I'll share a brief definition of each tool followed by a couple of suggestions for its use. Realize that creativity is always your best friend when using any of them.

Thank You and Goodbye

For use when releasing anything from your physical, mental, or emotional place and space. Throwing something out of your life generally has enough emotional momentum that it could ricochet back on you. Saying, "Get the hell out," is generally not as effective as, "Thank you," and, "Goodbye."

Speak to the habit, emotion, challenge… whatever it happens to be.

Invite it to let go of you as you let go of it.

You will be surprised who was holding onto who when you do this!

The dialog can go something like this:

I want to thank you for being my loyal and constant companion. When I had no one else I could always count on you to be no more than a thought away.

We have been through a lot together and I want to tell you thank you. I am ready to live my life without you now and I invite you to walk through that door. You are free.

It may surprise you when anger… stress… resentment… will take only half a breath and reply, "You mean I can leave? Really? You are going to let me go? Thank you!"

Imagine a door. Open it. Say thank you, then say goodbye. Invite the one leaving to have a good life and be transformed into something beautiful.

Intensity Dial

You can keep your intensity dial with you at all times. Ask your hypnotist to install it into the palm of your non-dominant hand (or anywhere else you choose). Its purpose is to give you the control to turn up or turn down the intensity of any moment, as you choose, for any necessary purpose.

The knob can roll to a higher or lower position. Mine is placed in the palm of my left hand and I run my fingers across with my right hand to turn it up or down. No one has ever noticed that I am rubbing my hand in a circular motion. It is subtle and it works wonders.

If you find yourself to be tired and you need a few moments of focused energy, turn it up.

When someone irritates you and there is not a better solution at your immediate control, turn the irritation down.

If the information being presented is important and you do not want to forget the crucial points, turn up your awareness to recall what you require.

Think of the things in your life that could be more enjoyable if you could turn up your personal response. Think of the times in your life when you felt like you just needed a break. This intensity dial can turn down the volume as well.

"That Was Easy" Button

This is another one for the center of the palm of your hand. Its purpose is to activate your willingness to take a break when what you are dealing with seems harder than it needs to be. It is for those moments when you think, "Man, there must be an easier way to do this."

When you need to see things from a fresh perspective, and you are willing for it to be easy, push your button. This one may take your subconscious a moment, as she reprocesses your current situation and sends an alternate option into your thoughts. Not because she is slow but because you have been ultra-focused and she needs to break through that frustration with a new idea.

After using your "That was easy button," be sure to acknowledge and thank that part of you who helped you grab onto something from a new angle or perspective.

Focus Ring

How many times would it be nice to (even if for just a moment) focus on *one thing* and get it either clearly configured or completed? The focus ring can be made of any material your situation or imagination requires. Do you need it to be rigid? Or would something amazingly flexible like silicone be best? Should your ring come with a sound barrier or a baby monitor? It does not matter. You and your subconscious will know how best to create your space.

Choose the object of your focus and place it inside your ring, then activate it for a number of minutes or the duration of the project. Once activated you are free to focus without the distractions from outside the ring. Conversations will not bother you, ringing phones do not concern you. You can set it so if you are waiting for a particular call then you will notice, but otherwise remain focused and undisturbed.

This is especially helpful for those who have something that must be completed on a deadline, but feel like the distractions keep you from getting it done. This one is also terrific for students getting ready for a test.

Cottage of Memories

The cottage of memories really does need to be set up with the assistance of your hypnotist. It is a rather complex mind game. Once established it can be modified at will.

The moment will come when we realize that if we could just clean up some of our memories, the time surrounding the events would become clear, giving us a totally different perspective.

This cottage has many rooms. The memories in each are invited to be washed clean. There is no need to stop to examine each as they go into the washer. Let go of all that show up—real, fact, fiction, imagined, or misunderstood—they're all ready for a good cleaning. When they are returned to the room, all of the crud and assorted extras have been removed and you can then look at your memories from an objective position of "What else was going on at the time?"

As a subject I go into my cottage frequently, I wash off a memory or an issue, asking for clarity and the gift of seeing what I had missed up until now. This one is more than worth the energy to create and perfect.

Healing Pool

Some people like being in water, some do not. This is for the ones who do. The pool can be a hot tub, a hot spring, or anything in between. The point is that the water heals. The swirling water is invited to flow to you, through you, around you, beside you. As it circles, the water washes away and removes anything… everything that keeps you from having the life you desire. As it swirls it is also continually being purified so that the old is gone.

You can also play with the color of the water depending on what makes you feel the best. For some that will be ocean blue, or fresh crystal clear, or a river steam. I've had a client who created the Pool of Bethesda, and another a mud bath. Both came out new and improved.

The powerful gift is recognized when you step out of the water and the healing pool allows you to leave behind all the impurities. It is a great tool when you just don't feel well. It does not take the place of medical care, but does give you an over-the-counter boost.

Picture Frame

The picture frame is a storage space for things which are better remembered at a distance. Not forgotten, but not in-your-face memories. This is not a tool for the really big-bad things in life, but rather for the irritations that are better put behind you.

Memories are usually brought forth in vivid color. When a memory is placed inside a frame, then invited to fade to black and white, the resulting image also fades its emotional attachments. Then you hang the frame on the wall behind you so it is no longer in front of you. To look at it again, you would have to make a clear decision to turn around, at which point seeing it is your choice.

Calm Me Down

We never know when something will toss our world into complete panic, when a calm cool moment would be the best logical choice. Those are frequently the times when stress and anxiety kick in at full speed.

Take a deep breath. Place your thumb and forefinger together, and say, "Calm me down."

This is a clear invitation for your subconscious to show up in force, to bring your system the boost you need to literally settle down and relax. Repeat as often as you deem necessary. This is not a once-and-done choice. Since you have your hands with you at all times, you can use it at will.

Scripts and Online Recordings

Proviso: You get out what you put into it.

Our world is flooded with a multitude of written and recorded hypnosis information and trance opportunities. Everyone has an opinion and all are usually valid.

One affordable way to experience hypnosis is through vast online libraries which are available either free or for a fee. Online hypno (for the most part) tends to be less expensive than in-person one-on-one sessions. Just be careful. It comes to you with a message created for a wide audience.

Tap into Subconscious's knowing so that the messages received are for your highest and best interests. When I first began my hypnotic weight loss journey, I found excellent resources from a couple of hypnotists who specialized in online downloads. Many are Internet-savvy and have the skills to reach out to a mass audience with precision, with a message that truly changes lives for the better.

It is also very common to receive a recording following a one-on-one session to reinforce a message you have already received. This is a continuation to the consultation you received while in session. A recording such as this is excellent to assist you to establish a fresh perspective for a desired new habit or behavior.

Now let's talk for just a moment about the *crap* that is out there.

My first red flag is usually when the hypnotist's voice is monotone and seems to be trying too hard to sound "hypnotic." When you need to listen to the sound of a voice and follow simple instructions, it's hard to do when the voice gives you the feeling the guy is creepy. If the voice makes you uncomfortable, stop. Your subconscious has a strong filter. Why subject her to having to override a drone?

A second red flag would be watching a video that uses a spiral pattern, trying too hard to draw you into trance. I find this one is closely connected to the first… a creepy voice with a pulsing screen. UGH!

Also be wary of downloads (especially if you are paying for them) that are a canned message… and somewhere in the middle you're given two minutes of focused attention on buying a copy of the next product for another issue or challenge.

You could instead listen to a beautiful sunset on the beach, walk in the woods, or lay back and watch the clouds form.

There are also scripts. Scripts are a mainstay in the world of hypnosis. It is powerful when a message can be duplicated and shared—regardless of who is delivering it—simply because the choice of words and the placement of emphasis is already determined by someone who has spent significant time getting it right.

When a hypnotist reads a script it is called "patter." When you read it yourself your subconscious will get 100% of the message and share with you what impact is available. How often have you read an inspirational book and immediately known you just received a potent message? Written words, in addition to those spoken, are potent, powerful, and personal if you willingly accept their ideas to positively change your life.

Just be careful. If it does not feel right, then stop. If the message is outside your comfort zone, then stop. If your first thought is, "This guy is an idiot," he is probably not someone you want wandering around in your mind.

Epilogue

I have dedicated this book to sharing with you what hypnosis can and does accomplish from the subject's point of view. I have never read a book that focuses on the effects of the life changed during the process of living in the realm of partnering with the subconscious mind. I am just the lady to do that.

I recently taught a class about the hypno subject's experience and told everyone clearly and very plainly that you absolutely 1000% can NOT get stuck in hypnosis. It is a by-choice, consent state of being. It is a connection with the subconscious on a real life level that transforms how you live, sleep, eat, and love. So, no, you can't get stuck... but why would you ever want to leave?

I often joke that if anyone ever tried to remove all my hypnotic suggestions and triggers I would kick their ass.

My life is *better*. My life is *PHENOMENAL* thanks to the new pathways my minds have created together.

I am richer, fuller, and more complete because I have come to know and appreciate all of me. I have opened my heart and mind to expand beyond my preconceived limitations and boundaries.

One of the most powerful components of this journey has been understanding that I don't know it all. The excitement of exploration and discovery sets up an almost insatiable desire for living more of life to its fullest.

It has been my pleasure to share from my heart to yours. Many of my stories leave room for open-ended curiosity. What happened next? What will happen in the future?

Will you join me on the journey?

Acknowledgments

I certainly did not make this journey alone. These past few years have been surrounded by phenomenal hypnotists. I would like to give a heartfelt thank you to Larry Lambert, Todd Stevens, Jerry Kein, Laura West, Billy Shilling, Robert Otto, Ina Oostrom, James Ramey, Sheila Granger, Sean Michael Andrews, and Ines Simpson.

I also appreciate the contributions of the following special people in my life: Demi Stevens, Tammy Stephens, Dan Leavey, Megan Yasenchak, and D.L. Glass.

About the Author

Sondra Lambert is a graduate of the Omni Hypnosis Training Center® and co-owner of Galaxy Hypnosis of Crofton, Maryland. She is certified by:

- National Board of Hypnosis Education and Certification
- National Guild of Hypnotists
- International Association of Counselors & Therapists

Connect with Sondra:

HelloSubconscious.com
GalaxyHypnosis.com

Certification Training Available Through:
http://www.omnihypnosis-dc.com/

Free audio download at: HelloSubconscious.com

In praise of Sondra Lambert:

In Trance proves that hypnosis can help you live a happier and healthier life. Sondra Lambert shows the therapeutic side of hypnosis—a welcome change from the common "entertainment" hypnosis most people are familiar with.

Sondra is a great example of someone who can deal with whatever life sends her way. The inner peace she's gained from hypnosis allows her to handle any situation with grace and composure. I've recommended her practice to friends and family and I'll be buying this book for them.

~Michelle Cormier, Bowie, Maryland

In Trance is riveting and filled with experiences of enlightenment.

Sondra is a woman who shares her heart with all who need love and caring. I was in her office crying uncontrollably, and she spoke to me softly and said, "I got you."

Working with my subconscious, we discovered I was missing my dad. Through hypnosis she helped me say goodbye, and gifted me with moments of clarity on memories that had been forgotten.

In Trance is such a compelling book, filled with different perspectives from both client and hypnotist. Sondra Lambert is special and unique. In this book you can feel all the love and joy she has in her life and how it's been transformed through hypnosis.

~Tammy Stephens, Gerrardstown, West Virginia

IN TRANCE is both fascinating and inspirational. It's the first book I've read that explains hypnosis from the patient's point of view. By the time I finished reading the first ten chapters, I was so intrigued that I contacted Ms. Lambert to set up an appointment. I hoped she could help me resolve some issues that I've had since childhood.

My first impression was one of a vivacious woman, filled with love for life—and barefooted. Yes, she was barefooted as she sat in the chair across from me and explained her method of hypnosis. Within minutes, I was relaxed and placed my complete confidence in her. Through hypnosis, Ms. Lambert placed me in trance, and took me on a journey that sent me down a path of self-healing.

In Trance is a "must read" if you have ever considered the benefits of hypnosis as a tool for healing, for communicating with your subconscious, or for achieving a goal that has been unreachable. The possibilities are endless.

~Terrie McClay, Chestertown, Maryland